Simply Living for Him:
A Devotional for Less Clutter and

More Joy

Scripture taken from the New King James Version®. Copyright © 1982 by Thomas Nelson.
Used by permission. All rights reserved.

Designed by Farmhaus Studios
Published by Simply Living for Him

For more information visit www.simplylivingforhim.com

Karen DeBeus has been ministering to women for over a decade through her ministry, Simply Living for Him. She is learning to live more simply and keep God at the center of it all. She is a best-selling author, speaker, and podcaster. She speaks nationally and recently was a speaker for the Family Bible Conference in Washington, DC. Her passion is to help others clear the clutter from their lives, seek God first, and to encourage women and families to get in the Word every day.

Visit www.simplylivingforhim.com
to learn more about Karen and Simply Living for Him.

What people are saying

"God's ministry through Karen has encouraged and equipped me in ministry to my children and other ladies. The heart of Simply Living For Him has continually been Matthew 6:33, "But seek first the kingdom of God and His righteousness, and all these things will be added to you." May the Lord continue to bless the work of your hands!" ~Vickie

"Karen's love for Jesus, doing it all for Him, putting Him in front of everything, puts everything into perspective, I keep going back to her books to continue on the path of homeschooling Jesus' way because He has called our family to it and only with Him we can do it." ~Kate

"Without reading and listening to Karen's love of Jesus… I would have never known Him for myself. I am forever grateful to be apart of the Simply Living for Him domino effect." ~Danyelle

"God has used Karen so greatly to remind me of what's most important and where my focus should lie! She's such a Proverbs 31 pillar who has helped my heart, faith, and perspective stay on the right track! So thankful!"~ Dana

"Karen is a grace-filled, relatable, and intentional mentor who points us back to the gospel of Jesus. She writes in tangible ways to help us feel safe, capable, and loved by God. You will feel overwhelmed with peace and gratitude as you are reminded of how loved by God we all are. I truly appreciate her patient, understandable, and gospel-saturated counsel." ~Cheryl

IMPORTANT: PLEASE READ BEFORE STARTING THE DEVOTIONAL

It has been my desire to write something that will reach across the pages of a book and point you to Jesus.

As a woman who has been transformed by Jesus and can only attribute my life to his miraculous saving grace, it is my passion to not only share His love with others, but to encourage other women to get in the Word of God. The magnificent God who created the billions of stars in the sky, infinite grains of sand on earth, and the One who knows every speck of the vast universe, speaks to us through the Bible. Yet, many of us get caught up in our lives and aren't spending time with Him. We are a distracted society. We have let other voices become louder than His. Our lives and our hearts are cluttered.

The remedy for clutter and chaos is Jesus.

I believe the more time we spend with Him, the less we desire the things of this world. The result is a simpler life with less clutter and more joy.

This devotional is designed for you to be in the Bible first, before reading the actual daily devotion. We want you to read the Bible for yourself, spend time meditating on what the verses say about God and who He is, and let His Word take precedence over my words.

After working through time with the Lord, I then invite you to turn the page and gain some further encouragement by reading the devotion. It is my hope to give you some perspective, but never to replace or come before the Word of God.

There is nothing more important than spending time with the Lord. It is where true transformation takes place, and where true joy is found.

Together, let's have less clutter and more joy!

Ecclesiastes 3:11

Observation	Interpretation

Application

Ecclesiastes 3:11

He has made everything beautiful in its time. Also He has put eternity in their hearts, except that no one can find out the work that God does from beginning to end.

My Notes

Ecclesiastes 3:11

My Prayer

_____
_____
_____
_____
_____
_____
_____
_____
_____
_____
_____
_____
_____
_____
_____
_____
_____
_____
_____
_____
_____
_____
_____
_____
_____
_____

Ecclesiastes 3:11

A Note from Karen

Every human being knows deep within their soul they were made for more than this earth. From the unreached tribal warrior on a secluded island, to the corporate worker on Wall Street, everyone has a deep sense of life beyond this one. Even if they haven't figured out what it is yet, they are aware, either consciously or subconsciously of an eternal Creator.

One of my earliest memories is me as a four-year-old lying in bed in the wee hours of the night and pondering some pretty deep thoughts. I remember thinking there must be someone out there above us who knows every single thing that will happen. I remember thinking about the future and how it is determined already. There must be someone who knows all of it. I don't know if those are the normal thoughts of a four-year-old girl lying in bed, but they were so deep I remember them clear as crystal.

Only years later, now as a woman who loves and serves the Lord and devours His Word, I understand I was thinking about the sovereignty of God and His eternal existence. I didn't know it had a name then but I do now. I didn't know God personally yet, but in that moment, it is clear He placed a knowledge of Him within me.

Since we are made in God's image and God is eternal, He has set eternity in out hearts. We will continue to yearn for it, because it is within us. But we are living in this temporal world. So there is a tension that exists.

God transcends our time and space. He is all-knowing, all-powerful, and ever-present. And one day, we will be in eternity with Him. For now, we long for our home with Him. That is why at the center of every human soul, wherever they live, whatever their beliefs, they still have a knowledge of a Creator.

Eternity is something planted in every soul, knowing that there is more to this life than just waking up, working, collecting stuff, going to sleep, and doing it all again the next day. There is a something much deeper within us. We were made by a Creator, for a greater purpose.

So, yes, the answer to my question as a little girl. There *was* someone out there that knew it all. He knows every single moment of my life and every other life in existence at this moment and each one to come. Even my adult brain can't wrap itself around such thoughts.

God has revealed Himself to us. He has set eternity in our hearts. It is up to us to hear Him, respond, and obediently follow.

I am so grateful that the sovereign God of the universe makes Himself known to us. It is truly incomprehensible! From a little girl lying in her bed at night all the way to the dying century-old soul across the world, He makes Himself known.

As we live in a world that gets louder and louder each day, spend some quiet time with the One who created us for eternity and for His purposes. The world will get softer as His voice becomes louder and the only one that matters.

Romans 12:2

Observation	Interpretation

Application

Romans 12:2

And do not be conformed to this world, but be transformed by the renewing of your mind, that you may prove what is that good and acceptable and perfect will of God.

My Notes

Romans 12:2

My Prayer

_____
_____
_____
_____
_____
_____
_____
_____
_____
_____
_____
_____
_____
_____
_____
_____
_____
_____
_____
_____
_____
_____
_____
_____
_____
_____
_____

Romans 12:2

A Note from Karen

"What is God's will for my life?"
"What if I don't fulfill His calling"
"How do I hear His voice?"

Every one of us has asked these questions at some point in our lives.

Yet, we can't know His will without knowing Him. And we must know His Word in order to know who He is.

The word for transformed in this verse means "metamorphosis" or changing into a completely new being. We see it in the beauty of a butterfly. It starts out as a caterpillar and transforms into a beautiful winged and gracious creature. It becomes completely new. None if it remains the same. And the caterpillar doesn't transform itself, but has been designed by His Creator to do so.

Only God can create a completely new creature out of an old one. He does the transforming work in us. An essential part of that is done by the renewing of our minds. That transforming work is powerful.

The word used in this text for renewing (of your mind) is translated to "renovate." I remember the year we renovated a bathroom in our home. We didn't just throw paint on walls. We tore them down. We didn't just add a fuzzy rug to make the floor look nicer, we ripped up the floor. We gutted the entire bathroom. Built new walls. Installed a brand new floor. Nothing stayed the same. It was completely made new. We didn't decorate to make it look nicer on the outside, but we renovated to transform the entire bathroom.

God is working in us to make us brand new. He is tearing down the old and building up the new. We are to be set apart and holy. And that begins in our minds. When our thoughts are transformed so are our actions. Out of the renewing of our minds, we will think differently and act differently. God's transforming power will work in us. We can discern His voice.

And that caterpillar? I have read it can eat up to 27,000 times its body weight in order to sustain itself for that transformation. Can you imagine? But it takes *that much* to sustain the transformation.

Just as we must feast on the Word of God in order to renew our minds as God transforms us.

We used to walk with the world, sort of getting molded and conformed to blend in. To look like the crowd. But now we are set apart. Transformed and made new.

That is His will for us. To be brand new creatures who, by the renewing of our minds (in His Word), will be able to discern God's will and walk in His ways and not the world's. We will no longer desire the things of this world or blend in with it, but our lives will be set apart for Him. Completely transformed by His miraculous work within us.
To God be the glory!

1 John 2:15-17

Observation	Interpretation

Application

1 John 2:15-17

Do not love the world or the things in the world. If anyone loves the world, the love of the Father is not in him. For all that is in the world—the lust of the flesh, the lust of the eyes, and the pride of life—is not of the Father but is of the world. And the world is passing away, and the lust of it; but he who does the will of God abides forever.

My Notes

1 John 2:15-17

My Prayer

_____
_____
_____
_____
_____
_____
_____
_____
_____
_____
_____
_____
_____
_____
_____
_____
_____
_____
_____
_____
_____
_____
_____
_____
_____
_____

1 John 2:15-17

A Note from Karen

Our human flesh always desires the biggest and the best. And often we go after things that tempt us because we think if we can acquire more we will be content. But God tells us to be content with Him and not chase after the things of this world, which end up leaving us empty.

It was my first year of dance school and I was 10 years old. Our dance class was having a Christmas party with a grab bag. Each girl was instructed to bring in a wrapped gift without a tag. As we arrived, we placed our gifts in a pile and when everyone was ready, the teacher said on the count of three we were to run over and grab a gift.

From the moment I walked in the room, I had my eyes on it. Amongst all of the tiny boxes wrapped in shiny paper stood this tall mysterious gift that towered over everything else. It must have been three feet high! And I wanted it.

As girls went scrambling to grab their gift, I shoved my way to grab that three-foot-tall prize. And as my hands wrapped around it, I felt such a twinge of satisfaction, not to mention excitement, to see what was inside! It was by far the biggest and had to be the best.

As I tore off the paper, my excitement quickly disappeared. There underneath the shiny wrapping was a plastic Santa Claus lawn ornament. And it was clearly used! (It had the dirt to prove it!) My heart sank. Every other girl opened up a diary, stickers, nail polish... you know all the things a 10 year-old-girl in the 80's wanted!

I was mortified. When the teacher called on me to show the class my gift, I felt my cheeks burn red as the snickers and giggles filled the room.

I learned that year, bigger isn't always better.

In fact, God wants us to stop chasing after the things of this world and chase after Him. He doesn't want us fixing our eyes on big and shiny earthly temptations. Because when the thrill of unwrapping the paper is over we often end up empty.

I know I did.

Do you have your eyes on the biggest prize? Are you looking for contentment in things? What are you grabbing for?

When we are satisfied in Him and content with Him alone, we don't desire bigger and better. We don't grab for the things of the world. We have the most precious gift already. The one that satisfies for eternity. And we are content with the truly greatest gift.

Focus on the gift you have in Jesus today.

John 10:27-28

Observation	Interpretation

Application

John 10:27-28

My sheep hear My voice, and I know them, and
they follow Me. And I give them eternal life,
and they shall never perish; neither shall anyone
snatch them out of My hand.

My Notes

_____

_____

_____

_____

_____

_____

_____

_____

_____

_____

_____

_____

_____

_____

_____

_____

_____

_____

John 10:27-28

My Prayer

_____
_____
_____
_____
_____
_____
_____
_____
_____
_____
_____
_____
_____
_____
_____
_____
_____
_____
_____
_____
_____
_____
_____
_____
_____

John 10:27-28

A Note from Karen

Are you afraid of the dark? Do you have a nightlight to help you see in the middle of the night?

When we hear God's voice we should respond and follow. We know that is where our safety is found. We recognize His loving voice and He is our Light guiding us. Our eyes should be so fixed on Him that we don't look beside us or behind us, but only to Him. Otherwise, it is too easy to get distracted by the things of this world and follow after them.

Sometimes there are "false" lights that we follow in this world. Unfortunately, there is no safety there and those paths lead to destruction. That is why we must never take our eyes off of the true Light.

Awhile back, I was watching a nature documentary with my son and one segment talked about these turtles born on a beach somewhere in Asia. They talked about how incredible it was that the turtles knew by the reflection of the moon off the ocean to go toward the light and that would lead them to the water. There they would find safety and life. Their instinct told them to follow that moon's light reflecting off the ocean. Isn't that amazing? What an awesome Creator we serve.

Yet, in recent years there had been large cities built nearby this beach. Those very turtles were now hatching in the evening light, but instead of following the moon's reflection off the ocean, they were turning in the opposite direction, toward the city lights. Those "false" lights were confusing them and they didn't know which way to go.

Unfortunately, many of those baby turtles followed the city lights away from the ocean and it only led to their destruction. They were confused and distracted by the city lights and they turned away from the ocean and headed toward the city. Such a sad little story, but such a vivid picture of our own lives.

Do you get distracted by the things that look appealing and look like the way to life, but only lead you away from God?

Do you get confused and disoriented by "false lights?" What is guiding you in the dark? The Light of the God or a false hope?

In order to stay on course and not get distracted, we must fix our eyes on Jesus. Listen for His voice. Do not follow others first, no matter how enticing their words. We must remain in His Word and in prayer. And then follow Him.

God is our safety and security in a confusing world. Seek Him wholeheartedly. Then you will not be confused, as you listen for His voice and follow His light.

Philippians 4:8

Observation	Interpretation

Application

Philippians 4:8

Finally, brethren, whatever things are true,
whatever things are noble, whatever things are
just, whatever things are pure, whatever things
are lovely, whatever things are of good report,
if there is any virtue and if there is anything
praiseworthy—meditate on these things.

My Notes

Philippians 4:8

My Prayer

_____

_____

_____

_____

_____

_____

_____

_____

_____

_____

_____

_____

_____

_____

_____

_____

_____

_____

_____

_____

_____

Philippians 4:8

A Note from Karen

Where have your thoughts turned today? Worry? Fear? Gossip? Perhaps complaining? Have you dwelled on the things of God? Have you filled your mind with beautiful things or cluttered it with ugly things?

God's Word is full of truths. And those are the truths we should meditate on in a world full of untruths. There is so much negativity and dishonoring "stuff" that goes into our minds daily, and sometimes it is hard to discern truth anymore.

But when you get in God's Word, and fill your mind with truth, you are able to discern what is truly good among all the noise of this world.

I think of it like this. I love nacho cheese chips. I could easily sit all day and graze on them and before I know it, the entire bag is gone! (trust me, I don't buy them anymore, but there was a time...)

Anyway, do you know how awful I would feel at the end of the afternoon after I grazed on that junk all day? My body wasn't made to live on artificial and processed junk such as nacho cheese chips, so naturally upon eating an entire bag I felt sluggish and sick.

But imagine I spent the day grazing on fruits and vegetables, or those healthy green smoothies packed with nutrition? I'd feel great. I would have fed my body what it was made to be fueled with. Food that nourishes me.

The Bible is meant to nourish our soul. But when we graze on junk all day–the Internet...a scroll through Facebook, an hour on Pinterest, too much time on Instagram, we end up feeling discontent, full of clutter, and most likely guilty for spending too much time there.

So, today, choose to dwell on what is lovely, true, and praiseworthy. Choose to fill your mind with soul-nourishing words and not junk. Because what goes into your mind will flow out in your actions.

Choose well. Choose truth. Be nourished. Because a nourished soul will not be so easily distracted. A nourished soul is satisfied in all things lovey and pure.

Psalm 147:4-5

Observation	Interpretation

Application

Psalm 147:4-5

He counts the number of the stars;
He calls them all by name.
Great is our Lord, and mighty in power;
His understanding is infinite.

My Notes

Psalm 147:4-5

My Prayer

_____
_____
_____
_____
_____
_____
_____
_____
_____
_____
_____
_____
_____
_____
_____
_____
_____
_____
_____
_____
_____
_____
_____
_____

Psalm 147:4-5

A Note from Karen

Do you ever stop and think about how truly big and magnificent our God is? There aren't really proper words to describe Him. I mean we say He is big. We say He is majestic and above all other things. We say we trust Him.

But if we stopped to really think about just how great and magnificent He truly is, we wouldn't be able to truly comprehend Him. He is truly indescribable!

We were learning about astronomy in our homeschool and it just blew me away to really ponder how big this vast universe is. How utterly incomprehensible is the size of the stars, the planets, and the immense space out there. It is something our human brains just can't fully comprehend. And He knows every detail of it all down to the tiniest atom. After all, He created each and every part of it.

Part of our problem with getting caught up in the daily noise of the world is that we don't think enough about *just how big God is.* We don't think about the fact that He created the stars! And the stars are not just little twinkling lights in the sky we sing a song about as kids; they are immense objects in space and there are billions of them! And He holds each one in place. Perfectly.

Think about it–the very same stars in the sky right now were there thousands of years ago, and in the same places. There is such order and precision in the universe besides the fact that it is just so enormous. And God created it all.

When we take our eyes off our little universe we make for ourselves each and everyday here...and onto the bigger and greater picture: that the God who holds those stars in place also knows the details of your life...then and only then, does a peace and comfort come over us like no other.

I can't imagine a more comforting thought than the fact that the God who created the universe, that holds the stars in place, and controls the universe, also controls my life. If He can control all of that, why do I worry?

The only security we have comes from the One who named the stars and holds them in place. We don't control anything. God does. And that alone is exactly where I want to be.

All glory and Honor to Him!

Today, ponder just how big God is. Be filled with that comfort and rest knowing the One who created the stars is in control of your life and has filled you with everything you need.

Philippians 2:14-16

Observation	Interpretation

Application

Philippians 2:14-16

Do all things without complaining and
disputing, that you may become blameless and
harmless, children of God without fault in the
midst of a crooked and perverse generation,
among whom you shine as lights in the world,
holding fast the word of life, so that I may rejoice
in the day of Christ that I have not run in vain or
labored in vain.

My Notes

Philippians 2:14-16

My Prayer

_____
_____
_____
_____
_____
_____
_____
_____
_____
_____
_____
_____
_____
_____
_____
_____
_____
_____
_____
_____
_____
_____
_____

Philippians 2:14-16

A Note from Karen

How many times a day do you think you complain? Either out loud or in your mind?

Pretty hard to add it up, huh?

I mean, think about it. We spend a lot of time dwelling on what didn't go our way or how someone offended us. Or even the smallest things: the weather didn't turn out nice. The grocery clerk took too long. Our hair doesn't look its best. One after another, words of complaint and negativity flow out of our mouths.

Do you ever think of complaining as mental clutter? It is. When we complain, we actually operate from a spirit of pride. And it ends up cluttering our soul with negative thoughts, deeds, and actions.

Complaining keeps the focus on ourselves. We didn't get what we want or think *we* deserved. Someone else may have offended *us*. Things aren't going *our* way. It's always all about *us*.

We forget gratitude. We forget God has created us in a world with beautiful people for a purpose. We serve a loving Father.

When we act out of humility, which is a fruit of the spirit, instead of focusing on ourselves, we realize that we don't really deserve very much here on earth. We are all just sinners who actually deserve death.

The Bible says that no one is righteous. Not one. But because of Jesus, we have been saved from an eternity apart from Him.

How can we complain about the littlest inconveniences when we have been saved from the biggest punishment there is! We should be praising every moment, not complaining.

Our perspective changes when we operate from a humble spirit. From a grateful spirit. We don't grumble about what we think we deserve. Instead we focus on how good and gracious our Father is. We aren't distracted by ourselves with a cluttered spirit, but a focused and clear soul doing what it is meant to do: praising our Father.

Oh, and that person who offended you? They need grace too. We all do. Give it to them from a humble spirit and watch your soul be free from negativity.

Today, choose praise over complaining. Lessen the load in your mind and shine like the light you were created to be.

Proverbs 15:16

Observation

Interpretation

Application

Proverbs 15:16

Better is a little with the fear of the Lord,
Than great treasure with trouble.

My Notes

Proverbs 15:16

My Prayer

_____
_____
_____
_____
_____
_____
_____
_____
_____
_____
_____
_____
_____
_____
_____
_____
_____
_____
_____
_____
_____
_____
_____
_____
_____
_____

Proverbs 15:16

A Note from Karen

Why does everyone seem to have it better than me?
Why do they have a bigger house, a better house, nicer clothes, more beautiful things?

Yes, embarrassingly I have had those thoughts before. Have you?

We live in a world that equates stuff with success and things with happiness. So it is very easy for us to look at others and desire what they have. And worse, we wonder why we don't have what they have.

Oh, what selfish thoughts.

God doesn't always reward with riches. He may at times, but it is not a measuring stick for our spiritual life. Not even close.

I have friends who visit Haiti several times a year as missionaries. Time and again they have said upon their return, these are the happiest, most worshipful, and content people they have ever seen.

And they have nothing in terms of material. A meager home–I am talking about a hut, not even what we would consider a meager home in America. They lack fancy clothes, shoes, or any material possessions. Their church: It's not even a building. It is a gathering on Sunday mornings of hundreds of believers without even a bench to sit on. If they are fortunate enough, they have a tarp over their heads.

And guess what? Their service goes on for hours. No one is watching the clock! They sing praises with hands raised (there are no "churchy" rules about when to raise your hands, how to raise your hands, and when to say *Amen*.) They are fully worshiping with their whole hearts.

They have nothing in terms of physical. But they have everything in Jesus. And they know it.

Do you know it?

Do you know you have *everything* in Jesus? Today remember, the stuff you have will mean nothing without Jesus. It is better to have nothing with Jesus, than to have great riches without salvation. Salvation though Christ is the greatest treasure there is.

Acts 2:46-47

Observation	Interpretation

Application

Acts 2:46-47

So continuing daily with one accord in the temple, and breaking bread from house to house, they ate their food with gladness and simplicity of heart, praising God and having favor with all the people. And the Lord added to the church daily those who were being saved.

My Notes

Acts 2:46-47

My Prayer

Acts 2:46-47

A Note from Karen

Have we complicated church?

Have we forgotten the simplicity of community? Have we cluttered up our sanctuaries and our schedules in the name of fellowship and programs?

In this passage it says, *The Lord* added daily to those being saved. Did you read that carefully? Not...our music at church, our coffee, our programs.

The Lord added daily to those being saved. Not our efforts. Not our work. Only the Lord. Anything we do is because of the Lord. He is the One who equips the saints for His work.

But so often we think if we get more people in the door of the church, that equals being saved. The important things to see in this passage are they continued with one accord and broke bread. They had gladness and simplicity of heart. And they praised God. And they had favor.

Simplicity of heart. Not the church decor or the church building even. Simplicity of heart.

We must remember that the Lord does the saving work. And our job is to be of one accord, break bread, be glad, and praise Him.

I'll never forget the first person I met who truly introduced me to Jesus. She had all of the above. She invited me to her home, broke bread with me, and literally sang songs of praise about Jesus. I was in awe. I had never met anyone like her. She didn't introduce me to Jesus in a fancy church service or an outreach program. It was in her home with the purity of heart for Jesus. And in turn, Jesus saved my soul. And as a result, who knows how many more through her or me have heard the Truth?

The saving of many souls. It is not about us, but about the Lord adding to the church. When we authentically and purely walk with Christ, others will truly see Him. They won't be distracted by the glitz and glam...but by a pure heart sharing Jesus.

So while we need churches and we need community, don't be confused about what is really saving souls. The Lord.

Today, choose to let Jesus work through you wherever you are. At church. At home. At work. At the playground. In the grocery store. Everywhere.

Break bread with others. Practice hospitality. Allow God to shine His light through you and accomplish the saving of souls. With simplicity of heart and praise, you can trust others will see Him in you. It doesn't have to be fancy. It just needs to be pure.

Proverbs 16:3

Observation	Interpretation

Application

Proverbs 16:3

Commit your works to the Lord,
And your thoughts will be established.

My Notes

My Prayer

_____

_____

_____

_____

_____

_____

_____

_____

_____

_____

_____

_____

_____

_____

_____

_____

_____

_____

_____

_____

_____

_____

_____

_____

_____

Proverbs 16:3

A Note from Karen

Did you ever have so much information about a decision that it was too much? And in the end, you never made that decision, for fear of making the wrong choice?

So much of our mental clutter comes from the abundance of information available to us these days. That abundance often leads to so much overload, we have trouble even moving forward in decisions. Some have referred to this as "analysis paralysis." We analyze every detail and end up paralyzed and do nothing at all. We are afraid of making the wrong choice.

For instance, you want to take a trip, so you go to the Internet and read every review of the destination, every bit of information you can find, and pore over statistics. You check every hotel and the surrounding areas. It all seems so overwhelming. You decide you will wait for the perfect time to take the trip.

Or how about when you want to make a purchase? You read all of the reviews, compare similar items, and analyze all the information you can find, only to remain paralyzed with fear of making the wrong choice.

Or perhaps you have a major life decision to make, and you think of every scenario of how it might turn out. And in the end, you are frozen in fear and never move forward.

We are a slave to information and it is chaining us to indecision instead of freeing us to move forward.

This causes stress internally and our cluttered minds shut down because we are now in full blown information overload.

But the Lord says to commit our work to Him and our plans will be established. He will determine the outcome. He is not going to lead us into confusion, but with discernment and peace.

Our job is to commit our work to Him. Our choices to Him. Our lives to Him. And trust Him with the outcome. He knows far more than Google ever will, and He is the One who is guiding us. Sure it is helpful to gain information, but when is it too much? And when are we operating in faith over fear?

God is all-knowing. He has more information and wisdom than the world has to offer. We can have peace knowing He is leading us to establish our lives and our purposes. He created us for His purposes.

The Lord wants us to move forward in faith and not fear. When you commit your work to Him, you do not need to fear the outcome. He is already there working all things for good.

Right now, commit your work to the Lord– your decisions, your plans, your life. And Let your plans be established by Him. Walk in peace and watch the outcome unfold, for His glory.

Luke 1:46-55

Observation	Interpretation

Application

Luke 1:46-55

The Song of Mary
And Mary said:
"My soul magnifies the Lord,
And my spirit has rejoiced in God my Savior.
For He has regarded the lowly state of His
maidservant;
For behold, henceforth all generations will call me
blessed.
For He who is mighty has done great things for me,
And holy is His name.
And His mercy is on those who fear Him
From generation to generation.
He has shown strength with His arm;
He has scattered the proud in the imagination of
their hearts.
He has put down the mighty from their thrones,
And exalted the lowly.
He has filled the hungry with good things,
And the rich He has sent away empty.
He has helped His servant Israel,
In remembrance of His mercy,
As He spoke to our fathers,
To Abraham and to his seed forever."

My Notes

Luke 1:46-55

My Prayer

_____
_____
_____
_____
_____
_____
_____
_____
_____
_____
_____
_____
_____
_____
_____
_____
_____
_____
_____
_____
_____
_____
_____
_____
_____
_____

Luke 1:46-55

A Note from Karen

When was the last time you truly praised? I mean, wholeheartedly praised the Lord for who He is. Not just what He does.

A heart of praise is one key to living simply. A heart of praise directs us to Him and away from the stuff of this world.

We are quick to throw around "praise the Lord!" and praising Him for answered prayers. We praise Him when things go our way.

But do we praise because we can't help ourselves? Because the praises of our lips can't be contained? Because it pours out of our soul by nature?

Mary's praise in this passage is so beautiful. Her soul magnifies the Lord! Isn't that spectacular? Mary lists all these amazing things the Lord has done, not just for her, but because of who He is and what He has done for all.

He has provided. He is our strength. He is holy. These things point to **who He is** and not just what He does.

We often think of blessings as the little things each day we "get." But what about who He is?

A Savior who spoke to our ancestors. He filled the hungry. He showed mercy. He saved lives and has done magnificent works from generation to generation.

It helps us to truly simplify when we praise. When we dwell on His magnificence, we realize how much we have in God and how little we really have in this world.

Are you praising like that? Are you praising Him for who He is?

He is majestic, faithful, and wonderful. He is a good Father, a merciful one, and gracious. He is all-powerful. All-knowing. He is loving and kind. He is gentle. He is Truth. He is our everlasting and eternal Hope.

Focusing on who He is, transforms our thinking from ourselves to a holy God.

So today, praise the Lord wholeheartedly. Remember Who He truly is and all He has done. Then sing a song of praise and watch the things of this world become less and less important as you magnify the One and Only!

Hebrews 12:1-3

Observation	Interpretation

Application

Hebrews 12:1-3

Therefore we also, since we are surrounded by
so great a cloud of witnesses, let us lay aside every
weight, and the sin which so easily ensnares us, and
let us run with endurance the race that is set before
us, looking unto Jesus, the author and finisher of
our faith, who for the joy that was set before Him
endured the cross, despising the shame, and has sat
down at the right hand of the throne of God.

My Notes

Hebrews 12:1-3

My Prayer

_____
_____
_____
_____
_____
_____
_____
_____
_____
_____
_____
_____
_____
_____
_____
_____
_____
_____
_____
_____
_____
_____
_____
_____
_____

Hebrews 12:1-3

A Note from Karen

What things entangle you these days and hinder your walk with Jesus?

For many of us it may be jobs, money, relationships, and even sin. You name it. And it can hold us back from running our race well.

But there is nothing new under the sun, and many of the issues we deal with today have been dealt with over thousands of years, all the way back to Bible times. Although the times were different, the themes of struggle and sin have followed mankind since the Fall.

But God has a race marked out for each one of us, and we must fix our eyes on Jesus and throw off those things that are distracting us. Jesus Himself endured a death on the cross because he had the joy set before him of fulfilling His father's will.

Can you have that kind of joy? Can you choose to fix your eyes on Jesus no matter what attempts to pull you down? Can you throw off every thing that tries to slow you or drag you out of the race?

You can. And you will. With Jesus. Generations of saints have gone before us. What an example of faith. We aren't the first to struggle. And we won't be the last.

A runner in a race never wears bulky clothes. They know in order to run and to run fast they must be as light as possible. They wear the lightest weight shoes and sleek activewear made for running fast. Imagine running in heavy steel-toed work boots, a wool coat, or denim jeans? That's what sin and those things that entangle us do. They hinder our race and slow us down.

What things are dragging you down? What is keeping you from running well? What is hindering you in your race?

Choose to run with a light load. Get rid of clutter and chaos distracting you from keeping your eyes on Jesus. He is cheering you on. Just as others have gone before you.

So choose not to allow anything into your life that isn't helping you in your race, and choose to run fixed on Jesus.

When you start to feel weighed down by the things of this world, simply look to Him and remember, you are not alone. Others have run this race and have endured with Jesus. And so can you.

2 Corinthians 5:1

Observation	Interpretation

Application

2 Corinthians 5:1

For we know that if our earthly house, this tent, is destroyed, we have a building from God, a house not made with hands, eternal in the heavens.

My Notes

2 Corinthians 5:1

My Prayer

_____

_____

_____

_____

_____

_____

_____

_____

_____

_____

_____

_____

_____

_____

_____

_____

_____

_____

_____

_____

_____

_____

_____

_____

_____

2 Corinthians 5:1

A Note from Karen

We spend an entire lifetime in our physical bodies. Many of us care for them quite well. We plan our meals, eat healthy, and follow the newest diet promising optimal results. We go to the gym. We make ourselves stronger. We want to keep things running smoothly as long as possible.

We also do all we can to make them look appealing. Makeup, hair styles, and the newest clothes. Some even alter themselves surgically to remain beautiful.

We spend a great deal of attention on our bodies. I mean, after all, we will spend our entire lives living in them. That could be up to ninety years for some of us. That is a long time to spend in a residence.

And then there are our earthly homes. We keep up with the Joneses. We care so much about the aesthetics of our homes. We have entire TV channels dedicated to showing us how to make them bigger and better and more beautiful. We spend enormous amounts of time and money and stress on investing in them to beautify them, to renovate them, and to make them a sanctuary.

And really, at any time, that home we are working so hard to make perfect can be destroyed. We see it all the time around us. House fires destroy. Tornadoes steal an entire life's possessions in a split second. A hurricane washes a home away in an instant.

And just as a home can be washed away or burned down, a body can be taken in an instant as well. And inevitably, no matter what, that body will continue to break down the older we get until some day it will perish. It will no longer house us. None of us can avoid that outcome.

But what about eternity? Ninety years in light of eternity is barely a drop in the bucket.

All that time, energy, and money spent is gone.

But our heavenly home can not be taken away from us. It is an eternal residence from God, not built by us, but by Him. Imperishable and eternal.

So then why do we strive for these earthly tents ? Yes, we are to be good stewards of what we have, but have we gone beyond stewardship, into idolatry?

We idolize the house and the body. We have bought the lie that this world is our home when in fact we are just passing through as we head toward our eternal home.

If we focused as much on our eternity and less on the temporal, our lives would be much simpler.

Today, focus on where you will spend eternity so you can spend more time building relationships, not homes. Spend your life investing in His Kingdom, not your own little kingdom. An eternal perspective will result in a simpler life. You will no longer strive to keep up with the Joneses, but to walk with God.

Ephesians 4:29

Observation

Interpretation

Application

Ephesians 4:29

Let no corrupt word proceed out of your mouth,
but what is good for necessary edification, that it
may impart grace to the hearers.

My Notes

Ephesians 4:29

My Prayer

_____
_____
_____
_____
_____
_____
_____
_____
_____
_____
_____
_____
_____
_____
_____
_____
_____
_____
_____
_____
_____
_____
_____
_____
_____
_____
_____

Ephesians 4:29

A Note from Karen

Choose grace over gossip every time. It is very easy to get caught up in foolish talk. Words spill out of our mouths before we realize it. In the moment, we speak unkindly toward others, especially those who aren't there and we can pretty quickly tear down another.

A humble spirit doesn't gossip because it is focused on the good of others. A prideful spirit loves gossip. It puffs up, even if it is only momentary.

We get a rise out of putting someone down to lift ourselves up. That is no way for us to model Christ.

Years ago I learned the hard way that my words matter. I sent an email to the wrong person. Vile, rude, and mean-spirited words about the person came pouring out of my mind and onto the keyboard and into that email. I intended to send it to someone else and instead I sent it to the very person it was about. I realized it as I hit "send." And there was no way to grab those words out of the Internet, as I knew they were being delivered straight to her inbox. There was the real me exposed for her to see.

It wasn't just because I got caught that I despaired. Yes, that was certainly part of it. But the shame I felt for being so two-faced. And really for just being so ugly. But, it taught me greater lessons I carry with me to this day:

Be the same with people, as when you are not with them.

And use your words to build up and to love. Not to tear down and spread discord.

I was just starting my walk with Christ at that time and He convicted me on this matter. I realized I certainly wasn't being a good example of Christ, with such negativity.

Gossipers are not trustworthy. Not only are they hurting the person they are gossiping about, they lose all integrity. I look at a gossiper and think, "Wow, if she said that about my friend when she is not around, I wonder what she says about me when I am not around?" Ouch.

Gossip brings about clutter. Soul clutter. It is negative and not God-honoring behavior. It may feel good for a moment but in the long term destroys. Others and yourself.

It doesn't even have to be gossip. *Any* negative talk, unkind words, complaining, foolish words. All of it is unwholesome. And none of it lifts up or honors God.

A humble spirit knows its place. Instead of seeking to be lifted up, it seeks to lift others.

Our words matter. Every word we speak has an opportunity to be heard. What will others hear from you?

Today, share the Gospel. Not gossip. Focus on using words to share the love of Jesus and honor Him with your words.

1 Samuel 18:14

Observation	Interpretation

Application

1 Samuel 18:14

And David behaved wisely in all his ways, and the
Lord was with him.

My Notes

My Prayer

_____
_____
_____
_____
_____
_____
_____
_____
_____
_____
_____
_____
_____
_____
_____
_____
_____
_____
_____
_____
_____
_____
_____

1 Samuel 18:14

A Note from Karen

What will it take for you to look back at your life and say you have achieved success?

A financially secure life? A top position at work? Sending your children to Ivy League college?

Maybe it's a luxury car? Or taking yearly trips around the world?

Or many of us may say that it's raising children to do well, or living a quiet and peaceful life, or just having enough to be content. Perhaps finding your soul mate, living without much complaint, and giving back to the community.

Two different views of success. And both valid in their own right.

While any of those things can be considered success and all of it can certainly be a part of success, true success can only be found in obedience to God's will *no matter where it takes you.*

In the trials and in the blessings, in the abundance and in the lack, success isn't measured by externals, but by our internal focus on the eternal.

True success is living in God's will.

This verse is translated in some versions to say, "David found success." You see, David behaved wisely and found success because God was with him. *He walked with God* and followed Him, seeking His will.

We often try to measure our success by tangibles. But a life that is following God and seeking His will above all can't be measured, and can't be contained. It is the eternal value of riches that last. It is the constant submission and surrender to God instead of our own will. It is the life lived completely for God.

You can have earthly success or heavenly ambition. Which will you choose to focus on today? If you only focus on outward measures here on earth, you will always try to reach for more.

Or worse yet, you will be measuring your worth by temporal standards.

But your worth is in Christ. Your life is found in Him. Measure your worth by His standards and you will have found the truest of all success.

Luke 3:10-11

Observation

Interpretation

Application

Luke 3:10-11

So the people asked him, saying, "What shall we do then?"

He answered and said to them, "He who has two tunics, let him give to him who has none; and he who has food, let him do likewise."

My Notes

Luke 3:10-11

My Prayer

_____
_____
_____
_____
_____
_____
_____
_____
_____
_____
_____
_____
_____
_____
_____
_____
_____
_____
_____
_____
_____
_____
_____
_____

Luke 3:10-11

A Note from Karen

Hoarding is a problem for many in our culture. The more we have, the more we hold. We are afraid to be without, so we control our stuff, and all of a sudden we find it controlling us.

Our possessions are not ours. All that we have comes from the Lord. So hoarding can lead to sinning. We keep for ourselves and add more and more clutter to our lives.

Several years ago we bought our dream home in the country. We wanted to live the slower and simpler life, get animals, and have our little piece of land to tend. The first year, we planted a large garden. We wanted to grow as much as we could and share our abundance with our new community and anyone who needed good healthy, homegrown food. We had dreams of a "garden food pantry."

The first year was successful. We set up a little table in front of our home with veggies from the garden and eggs from our chickens with a sign that said, "Free." My kids sat at the table, and when people passed we got to know them a bit. Many asked why the food was free. Eventually we printed out little cards which explained our mission. We shared that this house was not ours–it was a gift from God and we wanted to share our blessings with others.

And that is what we did. We hoped to share our food to nourish physically and share the Gospel to nourish spiritually.

This verse is painted on the walls of our barn. We want to remember that every blessing we have is not ours to hoard, but to share. Someone said to us once, "Do you know how much you can get for this food? You really should charge for it." But we don't feel that payment would compare to the payment of knowing that others heard the Gospel and had the opportunity to respond.

Do what you can in your life to share. It doesn't have to be elaborate. It can be as simple as paying it forward in the drive-thru for a coffee. Or any other simple gesture.

Because in the end, it isn't about *showing off* what you can share, but just *showing the love of God* through your actions. Through your kindness. Through your love. You never know the impact it can make.

Hold loosely to your things. Don't hoard. Don't try to control your life through controlling clutter.

Share. When we give, we trust the Lord to provide for our needs.

What can you share today? What can you let go in your life that isn't necessary?

After all, your treasures aren't here, but in heaven.

Proverbs 30:7-9

Observation	Interpretation

Application

Proverbs 30:7-9

Two things I request of You
(Deprive me not before I die):
Remove falsehood and lies far from me;
Give me neither poverty nor riches—
Feed me with the food allotted to me;
Lest I be full and deny You,
And say, "Who is the Lord?"
Or lest I be poor and steal,
And profane the name of my God.

My Notes

Proverbs 30:7-9

My Prayer

Proverbs 30:7-9

A Note from Karen

Have you ever forgotten the Lord because things were so good, you didn't really need to ask Him for much anymore?

Sounds like a horrible thought, but many of us do it.

My husband lost his job three times in our marriage. The first time, I was a newly married bride expecting our first child. Steve had only been working his first full-time job since graduating college about six months before. I was all set up to be a stay-at-home mom, fulfilling my dreams.

And then it all came crashing down.

Looking back however, we saw it as one of the most fruitful times in our lives. We became closer to God. When we had nothing, we realized just how much we truly had. Steve came to the point He knew God was all we needed. And from then on, our faith began to grow by leaps and bounds.

Sure, as a newly married couple with a baby on the way, it would have felt good to be prosperous and enjoy nice things. Instead, we couldn't even order a pizza. We had zero extra money. In fact we really didn't have anything beyond our essentials.

And we were closer to God than ever. We had no income, a baby on the way, and we discovered true riches.

Twice again in our marriage, Steve lost His job. And each time it brought us closer to God. We began to realize that when we became too comfortable, we stopped relying on God. Perhaps He needed to show us our need for Him, not just in the tough times, but in all times.

The reality is, we rely on Him in every moment. For every breath. For every thing. May we never have too much that we would distance ourselves from God or think we don't need Him.

Comfort often make us forget our provider. May it not be so!

What are you putting your security in today? Trust God to provide for your needs each day, and never let earthly comforts cause you to forget your heavenly provider.

Ephesians 5:15-16

Observation	Interpretation

Application

Ephesians 5:15-16

See then that you walk circumspectly, not as fools but as wise, redeeming the time, because the days are evil.

My Notes

Ephesians 5:15-16

My Prayer

Ephesians 5:15-16

A Note from Karen

Time. We never have enough. We constantly feel behind and we even dream of having more hours in the day. And all the while many of us our frittering our time away each and every day.

God created twenty-four hours in each day and He doesn't make mistakes. So asking for more time is saying God didn't know what He was doing there in Creation.

He gave us all the same amount of time, the same twenty-four hours, and the same seven days. How we use that time is essential to our walk with Christ.

Our actions are an overflow of our minds and hearts, and that includes how we spend our time.

Are we redeeming the time? Are we aware of the finite amount of hours we have on this earth?

Our priority should be to use them to share the Gospel and to honor God with the use of our time.

For those of us who never feel like we have enough time, we must look closely at why that is.

Where are we spending it? Are we wasting much of it? Are we truly aware of the purpose of our lives and our God-given time?

Are we busybodies? Are we spending much time doing, but not really getting much done? Even more, what we are we getting done for the Kingdom?

Time. We all have the same amount each day, but we never know when that time will run out. Be aware of that truth. It will change how you spend your days. Not just your hours, but looking ahead at the greater purposes of your time.

Evaluate where you are spending your time today. Make the most of every moment.

Redeem the time, and you will find you are not running out of time, but running toward the Lord.

Psalm 5:3

Observation	Interpretation

Application

Psalm 5:3

"My voice You shall hear in the morning, O Lord;
In the morning I will direct it to You,
And I will look up."

My Notes

Psalm 5:3

My Prayer

Psalm 5:3

A Note from Karen

Where do your thoughts turn to upon waking?

Your to-do list? Your worries of the day? Yourself?

Or maybe it's turning on the TV, opening up your phone, your tablet, or your laptop.

Before you know it, you have let the world speak to you before God has even spoken a word into your mind and your soul.

I used to do that. I'd wake up in the morning and immediately open my phone. I'd check my texts and email (which was usually junk anyway) and then scroll through Facebook.

Before I knew it, I was "running late." And I never opened my Bible. Worse, I hadn't even thought about Him.

I had every intention of spending time with the Lord later...*when I had more time.* But wait, didn't I just spend an hour in my virtual world before I even got out of bed? How dare I say I didn't have time?

Praise the Lord that He convicted me of this and over the years I have made a rule for myself:

No word will go before my eyes in the morning until His Word has gone before my eyes.

Even better yet: *No thought comes into my mind until I have dwelled on His truth through prayer first.*

We wonder why our world is so stressed and so discontent. We have filled our lives and our minds with so much it has taken away from our first Love.

We listen to other voices first and they have become so loud, we can't hear His.

In the morning when you rise...go to Jesus first. Not a thought, not a voice, or any other word, until you have spent time in His presence. It will change your life.

You were created to follow Him, not the world. Choose today to let no voice into your life before His voice has spoken.

Job 1:21

Observation	Interpretation

Application

Job 1:21

And he said: "Naked I came from my mother's womb, And naked shall I return there. The Lord gave, and the Lord has taken away; Blessed be the name of the Lord."

My Notes

Job 1:21

My Prayer

_____
_____
_____
_____
_____
_____
_____
_____
_____
_____
_____
_____
_____
_____
_____
_____
_____
_____
_____
_____
_____
_____
_____
_____
_____
_____
_____
_____
_____

Job 1:21

A Note from Karen

God is our giver. And He is also the one who takes away. He is the One who determines each and every moment of our lives. And what He gives us eternally far outweighs any material blessing here on earth. Yet, even those material things are His will.

When we realize all we have comes from Him and we really need nothing apart from Him, we will have true contentment.

My grandmother used to say, *"You can't take it with you."*

She had a true awareness of the fleetingness of stuff and the temporary joy it offered. Sure, we can enjoy our possessions, but if we let them define us and our joy, we don't let God define us. Our joy comes from Him alone.

When we recognize we came into this world with nothing, but we were created by the hand of God for His purposes, it is enough. And one day we will leave this earth and all of the earthly burdens we carried. And we will leave even those things that brought us earthly joy. They all will remain here as we go to our heavenly home.

I believe in that moment we will realize how we strived after such nonsense. We spent hours shopping for the perfect item. Or spent frivolously on things that didn't bring lasting satisfaction.

Imagine being in the heavenly realm worshiping God forever. All earthly joys will pale in comparison. We will see clearly how much time and effort was wasted on chasing after earthly possessions when we finally see eternal glory.

I want to have a glimpse of that now. To remind myself, *"you can't take it with you."* All that will last is joy in Jesus forever. A glory we can't imagine here. That will help lessen the clutter and distractions of earthly belongings.

Today, look around and remember, *you can't take any of it with you.*

Choose to live with the mindset that one day, all you see will fade into the background as you stand in His Glory. That will be the ultimate joy.

Psalm 9:1-2

Observation

Interpretation

Application

Psalm 9:1-2

"I will praise You, O Lord, with my whole heart;
I will tell of all Your marvelous works. I will be
glad and rejoice in You; I will sing praise to Your
name, O Most High."

My Notes

Psalm 9:1-2

My Prayer

_____
_____
_____
_____
_____
_____
_____
_____
_____
_____
_____
_____
_____
_____
_____
_____
_____
_____
_____
_____
_____
_____
_____
_____
_____

Psalm 9:1-2

A Note from Karen

What is your praise like these days?

It's really easy to praise half-heartedly. While your hands are lifted during worship service, your mind is thinking about other things. While you offer up a praise in the morning, your motive is often to get to the next task. You hear good news from a friend and you respond, "Praise God!" Then the next moment, you worry about something.

We all do it. We must recognize it and choose to praise wholeheartedly.

God is praiseworthy. Every ounce of our souls should continually offer praises to Him.

Not just when we feel like it. Not just when we are in the mood. Not just when He blesses us.

In all things.

And then, tell. Tell of our great God. Tell of His marvelous works. Not just the small things He does daily for you, but tell of His saving grace!

He saved your soul from death! He created this vast and enormous universe. Praise should be constantly flowing from your lips so those you encounter will want to know your God.

Are you praising? Are you doing it with all your heart, soul, and strength?

Enter into the mindset of just how marvelous He is, and you won't be able to stop it. It will be flowing from you continually as you rejoice in who He is and what He has done.

He has saved your soul!

When you are in the midst of this kinds of praise you won't grumble. You can't. And you won't add mental and physical clutter or unnecessary things to your life.

There is freedom when you are praising! A life of praise is so filled up on God, there isn't much room for anything else.

Today, choose to lessen the clutter and praise wholeheartedly!

Luke 10:38-42

Observation

Interpretation

Application

Luke 10:38-42

Now it happened as they went that He entered
a certain village; and a certain woman named
Martha welcomed Him into her house. And she
had a sister called Mary, who also sat at Jesus' feet
and heard His word. But Martha was distracted
with much serving, and she approached Him and
said, "Lord, do You not care that my sister has left
me to serve alone? Therefore tell her to help me."
And Jesus answered and said to her, "Martha,
Martha, you are worried and troubled about many
things. But one thing is needed, and Mary has
chosen that good part, which will not be
taken away from her."

My Notes

Luke 10:38-42

My Prayer

Luke 10:38-42

A Note from Karen

These days the life of Martha is definitely glorified. Take a look at Pinterest and Instagram and we see a world of Marthas. Those who can cook, sew, decorate, throw parties, and do it all with perfection are considered the epitome of modern day success in homemaking and womanhood.

You don't see many Pinterest posts of a woman, completely oblivious to how the photo looks because she is sitting at her Savior's feet.

Maybe her hair is askew, her makeup absent, but she has a glow about her that comes from being at His feet. And this is more beautiful than any of the picture-perfect details.

In a world that focuses on busyness and a picture-perfect life, Jesus tells us that Mary chose the better. And even more importantly, what she hears at His feet will not be taken away from her. What she sees in His eyes, can not be taken. What she feels in His presence, can not be taken.

The things of this world...even the picture-perfect...will all fade. The photos will fade, the things of this world will decay...but what is better...will not be taken.

Jesus is forever. His words are forever. His truths are forever.

Be a Mary today. It is truly the key to living simply and living a life with purpose.

2 Timothy 3:1-7

Observation	Interpretation

Application

2 Timothy 3:1-7

But know this, that in the last days perilous times will come: For men will be lovers of themselves, lovers of money, boasters, proud, blasphemers, disobedient to parents, unthankful, unholy, unloving, unforgiving, slanderers, without self-control, brutal, despisers of good, traitors, headstrong, haughty, lovers of pleasure rather than lovers of God, having a form of godliness but denying its power. And from such people turn away! For of this sort are those who creep into households and make captives of gullible women loaded down with sins, led away by various lusts, always learning and never able to come to the knowledge of the truth.

My Notes

2 Timothy 3:1-7

My Prayer

2 Timothy 3:1-7

A Note from Karen

We are living in the last days. Our world is becoming colder and colder to the things of God. Therefore, we must meditate even more on the truths of God and who He is. We must cling to those things or we will succumb to despair.

Often when I read the headlines or look around at the world, I am filled with such sorrow. It seems each day there is more evil filling the days. But I remember that humankind has always been depraved.

Think of ancient times and all the sinfulness that took place. There is nothing new under the sun. And until Jesus returns, we will live in a world that is wretched.

People want power. They want things. They are selfish. It is human nature. But we do not have to take part in it.

We were bought with a price and are redeemed. We are to be set apart and holy. We can live in this depraved world with a higher standard. Just because it seems hopeless some days, never means it is.

Jesus will return. And we will be with Him. But we must focus on the truth in a world that wants to deceive us.

This verse says people will always learn but never acknowledge. As a follow of Christ, you have the truth. Acknowledge it. Don't continue to search when it is right there. Live in it. Stop searching for answers. The answer is Jesus.

Are you tempted to be led away by untruths, other voices, or the things of this world? Today, turn away from the world and turn toward Jesus. Don't be held captive by new ideas or thoughts from others, but only be captivated by His Word, His truths, and His everlasting love.

Exodus 14:13-14

Observation	Interpretation

Application

Exodus 14:13-14

And Moses said to the people, "Do not be afraid. Stand still, and see the salvation of the Lord, which He will accomplish for you today. For the Egyptians whom you see today, you shall see again no more forever. The Lord will fight for you, and you shall hold your peace."

My Notes

Exodus 14:13-14

My Prayer

_____
_____
_____
_____
_____
_____
_____
_____
_____
_____
_____
_____
_____
_____
_____
_____
_____
_____
_____
_____
_____
_____
_____
_____
_____

Exodus 14:13-14

A Note from Karen

Imagine being chased and pursued with no way out, but you are told to stop. Don't move. Our instinct tells us that is crazy. We need to find a way out.

In a world that is busy and tells you to constantly be in motion, it is hard for us to read the words *stand still.* We feel that we must work to win. And that our successes come from within.

We think our strength comes from our inner-self. We can't imagine a solution to a problem that we can't see right now. We want to know how things will turn out or we want to control the outcome. We buy things to help us. We spend time looking for solutions. All the while, we forget we have the power of Jesus living in us. For each and every battle we face.

I love the picture in this passage. I mean, can you imagine? The Israelites are fleeing the Egyptians. They are on the run while being pursued by chariots and Pharoah's army. As they run, escape is on the horizon, and they are met with waves of the sea. How on earth could God bring them this far and have no way to escape? The despair they must have felt!

Well, sure by human terms, it looked desperate. The Egyptians pursuing them from behind. The sea right in front. There was no way out. Nowhere to go.

And then God tells them not to be afraid. He says He will deliver. I don't know about you, but in that moment, I probably would have questioned God. *What do you mean don't be afraid?*

There is no logical way out that I can see with my human eyes. No way of escape. And then God says to be still. That He will fight for us.

It's human to think we have all the answers and if there isn't a solution by tangible means, then there must be no solution.

Actually, the Lord is the One fighting our battles. The Lord is the One who knew the battles before we did.

And it isn't that we do nothing. In fact, it takes strength to have faith and take the step to still trust God in the midst of the battle.

When we take our eyes off of what we can do and focus on what God will do, the battle is won!

In fact, God already fought our biggest battle. And we did nothing. At the Cross. When humankind had no way out, He provided a way.

Today, be still. The Lord has provided a way out. He has provided victory through Jesus and continues to fight your battles.

Joshua 1:7

Observation	Interpretation

Application

Joshua 1:7

Only be strong and very courageous, that you may observe to do according to all the law which Moses My servant commanded you; do not turn from it to the right hand or to the left, that you may prosper wherever you go.

My Notes

_____
_____
_____
_____
_____
_____
_____
_____
_____
_____
_____
_____
_____
_____
_____
_____
_____
_____
_____

Joshua 1:7

My Prayer

Joshua 1:7

A Note from Karen

Prosper. We all want to prosper in life. Our culture tells us we need to go to school, get a degree, work our way up the corporate ladder, and we will prosper.

But God shows us differently in His Word. He gives us the key in these verses to prospering.

Stay on the path with Him.

The key to a prosperous life is to walk with God and stay in His Word and never deviate from it. We are to stay on His course, following His commands.

It is too easy in our world to get distracted off His path and turn right or left. It is too easy to change direction, especially with the abundance of information we have clamoring for our attention.

But God's Word tells us to stay the course. And wherever that leads us, we will prosper. It doesn't say we will get rich or famous. But we will prosper. There's a difference.

Some translations use the word "success." And success is knowing God's will and obediently following where He leads– whether to abundance or lack, mountains or valleys, joys or trials. We will succeed in all things, with Him.

Success isn't based on external conditions, but how we handle ourselves in all conditions.

Do you think about that as being successful or prosperous? Or do you equate earthly riches and material possessions with those things?

Today, remember you want to be prosperous in eternal riches. You can be assured if you follow God, do what He says, and stay on His path, you will prosper wherever you go.

Psalm 101:3

Observation

Interpretation

Application

Psalm 101:3

I will set nothing wicked before my eyes; I hate the work of those who fall away; it shall not cling to me

My Notes

Psalm 101:3

My Prayer

_____
_____
_____
_____
_____
_____
_____
_____
_____
_____
_____
_____
_____
_____
_____
_____
_____
_____
_____
_____
_____
_____
_____
_____
_____

Psalm 101:3

A Note from Karen

What we put in front of our eyes matters. What we watch. What we read. What we see. It is a direct line into our minds and into our souls. Do you ever think about that? What we see in front of us has more influence than we can even imagine.

When you choose godly things, you are fueling your soul. When you choose worthless or wicked things, (one translation of this verse says "vile") you are fueling sin.

Many of us find ourselves in front of some sort of news feed or media outlet for hours a day. The influence on our minds and souls is huge.

Scrolling through, ask yourself, "Is this bringing me closer to God or is it turning me away from Him?" Or, "Am I letting things pass by my eyes that are honoring and pleasing to God?"

Are those things distracting you from Him? Or are they pointing you back to Him? Does it build you up? Or does it bring you down?

This should help you discern what is good, honoring, edifying, and pleasing to the Lord.

On that same token, what we put out into the world also matters. When you choose to hit the "share" button, do you think about the eyes on the other end reading what you shared?

As one who works the majority of time online and shares words over the Internet, I am very cautiously aware of every word I write. I have often stopped myself from hitting "share" or "publish" because I have taken a moment to ask myself, "How will this build up? Will it cause negativity? Or strife?" Then I make my decision accordingly.

If we examine our hearts and motives, we will find the answer. Don't be so quick to share for a quick laugh. Or to make a point that may cause hurt feelings in the end.

What others put before their eyes matters too.

Today, remember to turn your eyes away from vile and worthless things. Set them on the Lord. And help others to do the same.

Colossians 3:1-2

Observation	Interpretation

Application

Colossians 3:1-2

"If then you were raised with Christ, seek those things which are above, where Christ is, sitting at the right hand of God. Set your minds on things above, not on things on the earth."

My Notes

Colossians 3:1-2

My Prayer

_____
_____
_____
_____
_____
_____
_____
_____
_____
_____
_____
_____
_____
_____
_____
_____
_____
_____
_____
_____
_____
_____
_____
_____

Colossians 3:1-2

A Note from Karen

Where is your heart and mind set these days?

At any given moment you are probably thinking about the to-do list, the kids, the calendar, the job, the home, and a myriad of other things. And at the end of the day, after mulling over all you have to do, you pray. And you probably ask the Lord for guidance or simply to bless your needs.

We have it backwards. We aren't meant to think about our earthly lives and then go to God. We are to think about our life with God and then live out our earthly lives.

Our lives are an outflow of our walk with Him.

Every part of your life is completely tied up in your eternal destiny and your salvation in the Lord. Your life is an outpouring of your new life in Christ.

So when you set your mind on things above, where Christ is, where your life is hidden with Him, you will have peace and joy and focus.

So often, we feel like our lives are chaotic and spinning out of control. That is because we aren't focused on things above.

There are purposes far above the daily grind. Our lives here on earth are but a vapor. But our lives with Christ are forever. Oh, what a glorious thought!

Today, choose to posture yourself with a mind set on the things of God before attempting to deal with the things here on earth. It will change everything.

A mind set on things above will be better equipped to deal with all that is here on earth.

Galatians 5:16

Observation	Interpretation

Application

Galatians 5:16

I say then: Walk in the Spirit, and you shall not
fulfill the lust of the flesh.

My Notes

Galatians 5:16

My Prayer

_____

_____

_____

_____

_____

_____

_____

_____

_____

_____

_____

_____

_____

_____

_____

_____

_____

_____

_____

_____

_____

_____

Galatians 5:16

A Note from Karen

If I could just get more organized.
If I could just get my piles of stuff under control.
If I could just get a better system in place, life will be smoother.

So many of us blame our disorder on the stuff around us. We never feel organized enough or as though we have things under control. We invest in new systems to helps us. Planners, organization methods, chore charts, meal plans. You name it. We seek after it to fix us.

For years I would try every organization method out there...gleaning all I could from blogs, Pinterest, and Facebook. I was on the search for creating a more organized and efficient home, filled with order and peace.

Chore charts, budget systems, personal planners, meal planners, school planners. I was always looking for a better way to get control over my life.

Yet it was never about the system. It was about me.

I do not have control. God does. All of those things offer a false sense of control if my heart isn't walking in the Spirit and letting Him control my life *first*.

Sure, systems can be helpful, but I was looking for the "be-all-end-all" that would create order and peace in my home. I wanted to feel in control of my life and was constantly searching for the next best way. I wanted the pretty bins, the color-coded life, where everything fit into neat little boxes.

I wanted peace and order. And that, my friends, is never found on Pinterest.

True peace and order comes from knowing the Lord, reading His Word, and following Him. Constantly striving to have the best system will not give us the true and lasting peace and order that comes only through Him.

It's not about how things look on the outside, but where our hearts are on the inside. Stop the need to search out every method of organization that ends with you still feeling restless.

Today, you can choose to stop relying on the things of the flesh and rely on God. He is the One in control of your life. He is the One who will give you the peace and order you desire.

Don't rely on the things of this world. Let Him lead. Be free of the need to control, knowing He is the One who controls all things.

Matthew 6:25-33

Observation

Interpretation

Application

"Therefore I say to you, do not worry about your life, what you will eat or what you will drink; nor about your body, what you will put on. Is not life more than food and the body more than clothing? Look at the birds of the air, for they neither sow nor reap nor gather into barns; yet your heavenly Father feeds them. Are you not of more value than they? Which of you by worrying can add one cubit to his stature?

"So why do you worry about clothing? Consider the lilies of the field, how they grow: they neither toil nor spin; and yet I say to you that even Solomon in all his glory was not arrayed like one of these. Now if God so clothes the grass of the field, which today is, and tomorrow is thrown into the oven, will He not much more clothe you, O you of little faith?

"Therefore do not worry, saying, 'What shall we eat?' or 'What shall we drink?' or 'What shall we wear?' For after all these things the Gentiles seek. For your heavenly Father knows that you need all these things. But seek first the kingdom of God and His righteousness, and all these things shall be added to you.

Matthew 6:25-33

My Prayer

Matthew 6:25-33

A Note from Karen

What do you seek first? Is it truly the Kingdom and the things of God? Or is it your own comforts, plans, and fulfillments?

Are you trusting God to provide for your needs, or are you focused on the things you want?

If we all truly believed what Matthew 6:33 says, we could eliminate much of the chaos and clutter from our lives.

I was just beginning my walk with Jesus back in 1999 and I opened to this passage. I had been going through a difficult time making decisions about my job. I was wrestling with how I would be provided for. And these words jumped off the page.

Suddenly it all made sense. God was my provider. My job was to seek Him and to follow Him. Up until that point in my life I had always tried to do things my way. And most of my focus wasn't on things of God but on me.

Where would I live? Where would I work? What would I do? How much money would I make? *Me. Me. Me.*

We live in a consumer-culture emphasizing the importance of clothes, homes, and food. We have twenty-four hour TV channels devoted to these things. We have Pinterest and Instagram showing us how to obtain all these things. The culture fosters an attitude of materialism.

And all the while God is telling us to build His Kingdom, not our own little kingdoms.

We do not need those twenty-four hour TV channels when we have a twenty-four hour guide available to us–*the Bible*. Do we go there first? Or do we let society dictate what we need?

This passage changed my life. Matthew 6:33 became my life verse. I base my family, home, ministry, and life on it.

Today, decide to seek Him first. Above all else. Go to His Word and listen to Him. Your life will become an outflow of your relationship with Him. The more you desire Him, the less you will naturally desire the things of this world. You can live with less distraction and less desire for "stuff" because you are focused on Him. Your desires change from the things of this world to the things of God.

When you follow Him, He will never ever fail you. He provides for your needs (not necessarily your wants) and you recognize your one true need is Jesus.

Today, seek Jesus above all. Your life will be changed as you desire Him first.

Hebrews 13:8

Observation

Interpretation

Application

Hebrews 13:8

Jesus Christ is the same yesterday,
today, and forever.

My Notes

Hebrews 13:8

My Prayer

_____
_____
_____
_____
_____
_____
_____
_____
_____
_____
_____
_____
_____
_____
_____
_____
_____
_____
_____
_____
_____
_____
_____
_____
_____
_____
_____
_____
_____

Hebrews 13:8

A Note from Karen

Trends come and go. We see it in fashion, our homes, and in every aspect of life. What is new will become old very quickly. Then it will come back in style. The funny thing is, who decides what is on trend?

We spend thousands of dollars updating our homes, only to have vintage styles come back. It is crazy when you think about it!

What if there were no trends? What if we just focused on the function of our homes and keeping them simple and perhaps beautiful in our eyes, without the latest fads influencing us? We would save a ton of time and money. We wouldn't be constantly in a state of renovation, decorating, and searching out the right pieces. We would be content with our home that functioned well and housed us.

The same holds true for fashion, or even what we eat. New fads come in and it's "out with the old and in with the new!" These things consume so much of our time, energy, and even money, as we change with the latest trends.

And the world is constantly changing its mind on morality. What was once immoral has now become moral. What was frowned upon twenty years ago is now acceptable and the norm.

Yet, Jesus always stays the same.

Praise God, He never changes, in a world that is so unstable. We can trust that His Word is true. He can not lie. He doesn't shift with the times. He doesn't change depending on what the culture "feels" or believes."

He is who He says He is. What a gift to have absolute truth in a world full of subjectiveness.

Compare it to math. Look at numbers and see unchanging truths. 2+2 =4. Always. It isn't 5 tomorrow because I feel like it should be. It isn't 5 next week because in my opinion it should be 5. It is always 4. Today, tomorrow, and forever. Just like Jesus.

In a world that confuses us with its constant morphing, we can stand on the absolute truth of God and His Word. It is trustworthy. It can only be true. I don't know how I would live without that unchanging truth to hold onto in a confused world.

We have the gift of knowing the absolute Truth. What was true at the beginning of time is true today and will always be for eternity.

Remember as you see the world around you shifting everyday, do not cling to the promises of a world built on its own truths. Cling to the eternal promises of the One true God.

Cling to Jesus. Today, tomorrow, and forever.

Philippians 1:21

Observation	Interpretation

Application

Philippians 1:21

For to me, to live is Christ, and to die is gain.

My Notes

My Prayer

_____
_____
_____
_____
_____
_____
_____
_____
_____
_____
_____
_____
_____
_____
_____
_____
_____
_____
_____
_____
_____
_____
_____
_____
_____
_____
_____

Philippians 1:21

A Note from Karen

The American Dream says dream big, achieve status, attain wealth, and live that picture-perfect life. The house, the white picket fence, and the kids and dog to go with it.

But what does God's Word say about how we should live our lives?

He says the first shall be last and the last shall be first. He says we are to store treasure in heaven and not on earth. He says we are to give what we have and not hoard for ourselves.

He says we are to lose our life to gain it.

Clearly, the American Dream make us focus on material possessions and external rewards. And for so many, the rewards never really fulfill us. We chase and chase and achieve the next level, but it never seems to be enough. It doesn't satisfy for very long.

Because we weren't made to be completely satisfied with the things of this world.

Sure, it may offer a temporary fix or short-term contentment. But very quickly, it wears off and we are on to conquer the next thing.

Jesus conquered all already.

You can stop trying to conquer. Stop trying to achieve. Stop trying to attain.

Certainly we can work toward goals here on earth and fulfill different levels of achievement. But when you know that life isn't just about all those things, and is all about Jesus, you will stop trying to find yourself in those things.

Instead, start striving for the things He created you for.

Eternity.

Your identity is in Christ. Not what you do or what you have. Those things are part of you but do not define you. They are part of your earthly life but you don't find your ultimate fulfillment here on earth.

Let go of the things of this world you think define who you are. You already have gained every thing you need in your heavenly residence. Your job on earth in this very short span of time you have been given, is to do all you can to share that with others, live out your faith, and grow closer in your walk with God.

Lose the things that are clouding your vision. Lose the things you are depending on to define you. And gain all that you already have in Christ and will last for eternity.

1 Peter 1:3-5

Observation	Interpretation

Application

1 Peter 1:3-5

Blessed be the God and Father of our Lord Jesus Christ, who according to His abundant mercy has begotten us again to a living hope through the resurrection of Jesus Christ from the dead, to an inheritance incorruptible and undefiled and that does not fade away, reserved in heaven for you, who are kept by the power of God through faith for salvation ready to be revealed in the last time.

My Notes

1 Peter 1:3-5

My Prayer

_____
_____
_____
_____
_____
_____
_____
_____
_____
_____
_____
_____
_____
_____
_____
_____
_____
_____
_____
_____
_____

1 Peter 1:3-5

A Note from Karen

A few days before Christmas we were out shopping– the stores were packed, the shelves were stocked, and people were all striving to find those last minute perfect gifts. Everything looked so shiny and inviting. Each aisle promised excitement and satisfaction. It was easy to give in to the temptation to spend and buy. Everything in sight held the promise of pleasure.

At that moment the energy was high. It was palpable in every store.

A few days after Christmas, we walked into those very same stores. The very same aisles. I was taken aback by the stark contrast. Just days before, what was so alluring and pretty was now a disheveled, hollow, and stark space. Most of the shelves were empty, but what was left, was a mess.

Those sparkly shiny objects? Now they looked different. They no longer were must-haves, but they were marked down to 90% off, just to get rid of them. No one was interested in them anymore. They weren't so exciting. Many were broken and tattered.

A stark contrast indeed.

Isn't that the irony of this world? We want. We buy. Things scream for our attention. They are inviting and alluring. Yet, what captivated us at first, fades away and becomes old in an instant. What was once coveted becomes a throwaway item. The anticipation, the joy, and the excitement of the pre-holiday rush melts into a heap of exhaustion. There's relief that it's over.

I always say, "This year's must-haves are next year's garage sale items."

Like the white glistening of a fresh snowfall. We marvel in its beauty, sparkle, and pure whiteness. Then just days later, we trudge through brown slush.

Everything on this earth fades. We can never hold onto it. Whether it is a new gift, fresh snow, or even the feeling we have at the beginning of something new. It all fades. The very things we anticipated so fully, pass by quickly and become memories.

We simply can't hold onto things of this life. We can't hold onto things that aren't permanent. We are always moving forward away from this earth and toward the one thing that will never fade–eternity.

Today, I encourage you to remember the transience of things. Yes, they feel good in the moment, but are they taking your attention away from the things that matter most?

Eternity is permanent. Nothing here can ever shine as brightly or satisfy us like the day we enter into His presence forever.

If you focus on that day it will change your perspective in the here and now. You will recognize the temporary joys here and await for the eternal glory in heaven! Amen?

Psalm 119:165

Observation

Interpretation

Application

Psalm 119:165

Great peace have those who love your law,
and nothing causes them to stumble.

My Notes

Psalm 119:165

My Prayer

_____
_____
_____
_____
_____
_____
_____
_____
_____
_____
_____
_____
_____
_____
_____
_____
_____
_____
_____
_____
_____
_____
_____

Psalm 119:165

A Note from Karen

A quick swerve on the road can have a devastating effect. It only takes a split second to veer off course if you take your eyes off the road.

Recently, this very thing happened to me. I looked down for a split-second because something fell, and my car began to swerve. I was jolted back and quickly directed my eyes onto the road, determined not to let that happen again.

Then I realized how much it is like our walk with Jesus. We are going about smoothly, then all of a sudden something of this world distracts us, and we get off course. We may even swerve into dangerous places. Or we feel out of control. Until we get our eyes back straight where they should be. On Jesus.

There are all sorts of things clamoring for our attention these days. Worry, idols, busy schedules, unexpected events, job, family. All of it can distract us.

Are you living a distracted life?

For me worry often distracts me. Or details about the future. Or details about the present. Things that are usually out of my control.

The Internet distracts many of us. Or what others are saying or doing. There are tons of things making noise and we have a hard time discerning what is true and right.

The enemy wants you to swerve and crash. But God wants your full attention.

Keep your eyes on Jesus and you will not be tempted to look away. Because the more you look at Him, the less your desire will be to turn away and succumb to the distractions of this world.

Get in your Bible. Know the truth. Spend time with Him. Things become so much clearer when your eyes are fixed firmly on Jesus. When that unexpected obstacle comes your way, you can easily steer right around it, knowing God is in control.

Choose today to set your eyes firmly in front of you. Live with a laser sharp focus.

Nothing in this world can ever deserve more attention than Him.

1 Peter 4:9

Observation	Interpretation

Application

1 Peter 4:9

Be hospitable to one another without grumbling.

My Notes

1 Peter 4:9

My Prayer

_____

_____

_____

_____

_____

_____

_____

_____

_____

_____

_____

_____

_____

_____

_____

_____

_____

_____

_____

_____

_____

1 Peter 4:9

A Note from Karen

In a media-saturated culture, it is easy to focus on making a house that looks picture-perfect.

The amount of time and energy spent on making things "look" perfect is astounding. Yet none of those things will go with us into eternity. We need to be investing our time, focus, and energy on what goes on inside those four walls of a house and building our family first. Relationships matter into eternity. Material possessions will perish.

I would rather people come to my house and forget the decor, but remember they encountered Jesus.

The most beautiful part of a home, is when it is filled with Jesus.

I remember when I first got married, all of my attention was on making the perfect home. I paid careful attention to details, and truth be told, I wanted people to admire my home.

I spent money I didn't have, time I didn't have, and energy I surely needed for other things, on shopping, planning, and decorating. The funny thing is, we didn't have much. We had a modest home, but I wanted it to be perfect.

Over the years, as I grew closer in my walk with the Lord and He led me to live a more simple life focused on Him above material things, my desires changed. When I invited friends over, it was no longer about me showing off my perfect place settings or the intricate recipe I found on Pinterest. It was about swinging open the door wide for all to enter and see the love of Jesus in our home.

Entertaining in our homes says, "Look what I can do." Hospitality says, "What can I do for you?" When we entertain it is about us. When we practice hospitality it is about our guests.

I would rather a guest come into my home and not notice the dust bunnies or dated decor, because they were feeling the love of Jesus in our home.

Are you building a house or a home? Today, choose to focus on using that home as a haven to serve others. Focus on how they feel in your home. And most of all, share the love of Jesus.

Psalm 34:8

Observation	Interpretation

Application

Psalm 34:8

Oh, taste and see that the Lord is good;
Blessed is the man who trusts in Him!

My Notes

Psalm 34:8

My Prayer

_____

_____

_____

_____

_____

_____

_____

_____

_____

_____

_____

_____

_____

_____

_____

_____

_____

_____

_____

_____

Psalm 34:8

A Note from Karen

Sometimes we need to be reminded. Life isn't for our comfort. The sole purpose of our life is not for God to make things easy or comfortable for us, or even pleasant all the time.

The sole purpose of our life is to glorify God. Even when things aren't comfortable.

Especially when things aren't comfortable.

I've been contemplating the term "blessings" lately. So many people equate blessings with stuff. Or with good feelings. You know, the "warm fuzzy" blessings.

I sign my emails, "blessings and joy." I say it when I end my podcasts. Yet, what do I mean by that? Do I mean God is going to answer your prayers and rain down "stuff "on you? Or is He going to give you an easy life? Do I equate blessings only with pleasures?

Actually no.

When I wish you blessings and joy I am hoping you have the ultimate blessing. Jesus.

We say we want to be blessed and we wish blessings on others, but we are already blessed. We already have the only blessing there really is–knowing Jesus.

If our prayers don't get answered our way, when we have nothing left in the bank account, when the doctor doesn't give us the answer we were hoping for–we are still blessed if we have Jesus.

And in Jesus there is joy.
No matter what swirls around us.

So may we not equate blessings with things. May we not equate what He has given us as the blessing. May we equate Who He is with the blessing. And what He has done for us on the Cross.

Because the truth is, if tomorrow He takes it all away, we are still blessed. And we can still have joy.

Because we have Jesus. He is our blessing and our joy.

What are you considering a blessing today? Where does your joy come from? If God didn't answer a prayer the way you hoped, does it change how blessed you are?

These are all things to consider as you walk with the Lord, loosening your grip on things, and focusing on the joy in Jesus.

1 Timothy 6:6-7

Observation	Interpretation

Application

1 Timothy 6:6-7

Now godliness with contentment is great gain.
For we brought nothing into this world, and it is
certain we can carry nothing out.

My Notes

1 Timothy 6:6-7

My Prayer

1 Timothy 6:6-7

A Note from Karen

Our emotional attachment to stuff often hinders us from throwing it away. And before we know it, piles accumulate, our basements and attics are overflowing, and we don't know how to let it all go.

Now I always say I am the opposite of a hoarder. If it is in my way, I may just throw it out! I don't like piles or how I feel when a room is cluttered. It adds stress and I feel myself getting anxious at the sight of endless piles of stuff.

But there are those certain things that are hard to let go. The sentimental objects. The baby things. The photos. The little things that seem trivial to anyone who isn't attached to it like you are.

So how do we let go of things if we are tied to them emotionally?

If you are hanging on to things because of a sentimental attachment then it may be time to evaluate. Are you letting your past clutter up your present? Are you trying to hang on to a feeling of the past, while it hinders your present or even your future?

We can have an emotion and a memory without hanging onto every single thing from the past.

We can't get caught up in stealing from our future or even our present because we are holding onto clutter from the past.

You have JOY in the present and a future glory to anticipate. Enjoy the memories without cluttering up your life now.

You can't take anything tangible with you from this world into eternity. Hold loosely to the earthly goods, especially those that cause overwhelm.

Today, fix your eyes on your treasure in heaven, knowing the objects here are temporary, but the emotions they stir and the feelings they provoke, are eternal possessions.

John 12:43

Observation	Interpretation

Application

John 12:43

for they loved the praise of men more than the
praise of God.

My Notes

John 12:43

My Prayer

_____
_____
_____
_____
_____
_____
_____
_____
_____
_____
_____
_____
_____
_____
_____
_____
_____
_____
_____
_____
_____
_____
_____
_____

John 12:43

A Note from Karen

As humans we have an inborn need and desire to be loved. We seek approval. We search for validation. And these days, the Internet often provides an instant balm to this need. A few "likes' on a post...or better yet, "loves" and we feel validated. We feel loved. Because a button told us so.

Often we don't even realize those little "likes" or "loves" (and hopefully not the dreaded "angry" face!) can really affect our mood. If we don't get the validation we are after, we might internalize it, feeling like nobody cares.

My friends, do not, I repeat, do not, let the Internet be your measure of worth.

Silly little likes on a post have nothing to do with your true worth.

As humans, though, our need for approval (and even better when it is instantaneous) fuels us to seek more of it.

But God's love for you reaches far beyond the reach of a social media post. You are the daughter of a King. Walk in a manner that is worthy.

Seek the approval of God and not man.

Choose to go to His Word when you are feeling "less than," and let your Father provide for your needs above and beyond.

And instead of puffing up your pride through an Internet post, you will be humbly at His feet, knowing that His love is all you need.

Today, ask yourself if you are seeking approval from others. If so, recognize that it is adding to a cluttered soul. But the joy, oh the joy, of knowing you need only to seek approval from the Lord. He is the One you are living for!

Isaiah 55:2

Observation	Interpretation

Application

Isaiah 55:2

Why do you spend money for what is not bread,
And your wages for what does not satisfy? Listen
carefully to Me, and eat what is good, And let
your soul delight itself in abundance.

My Notes

My Prayer

_____
_____
_____
_____
_____
_____
_____
_____
_____
_____
_____
_____
_____
_____
_____
_____
_____
_____
_____
_____
_____
_____
_____

Isaiah 55:2

A Note from Karen

Living simply is not about a cute minimalist lifestyle arranged "just so" for a photo.

A few years back, a missionary homeschooling mom in Kenya wrote me, and it stopped me in my tracks. She said:

"When I came across your page on Facebook I was so encouraged because I just don't see that focus on Jesus much anymore. It can be discouraging sitting over here on the other side of the world trying to share Jesus with others and I see other moms wasting their lives and kids' lives on so much junk!"

Now, I know how I feel when I see things that distract us daily. But I never imagined what it must look like to someone living over in Africa...sharing God's love as a missionary, and homeschooling...and to see how we are over here focused on so much nonsense. The perfect meal plan, Pinterest board, crafts, decor, gadgets, latest and greatest earthly pleasure, or whatever it is...

Imagine how we look, chasing after the things of this world, but claim the name of Jesus?

Let us not lost our focus. Let us keep the main thing, the main thing. This life is short. The time is precious. And our moments should matter for Jesus.

Yet, we are stuck in the middle of this noisy and distracting world with all its shiny pleasures. It woos us with its temporal goodness. And, in and of themselves, many of those things are good. It is okay to enjoy pleasures. We are meant to enjoy things, but there is a distinction between enjoyment and our happiness depending on them.

We must not seek things before Him. We can not live for the here and now, the picture-perfect life, and things that are superficial, and not live for eternity.

We are drowning in a sea of information, but losing our wisdom. We are attaining earthly success, but forgetting about eternal gain. We seek our own glory before His. We forget our purpose in life: to know Him and make Him known.

The more we desire Him, the less we will desire of this world. When we thirst for Him, those earthly pleasures don't seem so satisfying anymore.

A simple life, for me, weeds out the things that are hindering me from my one and only satisfaction in life. Jesus. Nothing more, nothing less. I want to seek after Him so much that I don't care what the world has to say about the next best thing.

May we continue to chase after the right things! May we stop feasting on the junk of this world and filling up on earthly pursuits while starving for Jesus. May we seek Him first so that everything else falls into its proper place. May our lives reflect Jesus.

Let's not waste our precious time as women on rubbish. Let's teach the next generation what is truly important.

Psalm 119:37

Observation

Interpretation

Application

Psalm 119:37

Turn away my eyes from looking
at worthless things,
And revive me in Your way.

My Notes

Psalm 119:37

My Prayer

Psalm 119:37

A Note from Karen

Many years ago I knew that my time with the Lord was lacking. I realized I awoke each morning and the first thing I did was open my phone, check my texts, emails, and scroll Facebook. Before I knew it, I was rushing because the day was already getting away from me. I approached my day with a mind set on the things of this world. I had let everyone speak into my day before the Lord had spoken into my day.

Then and there I made a rule. *Set no words before my eyes in the morning, until God's Word had gone before my eyes.* This meant that before I read texts or email, I would read the Bible. I didn't plan on having a study time early in the morning, but merely to read His Word first. To set my mind on things above before I tried to deal with the things of this earth.

That little rule I set for myself transformed my life. At first, it was something I made myself do, but before long, I began to desire His Word in the morning. You see, I had set an app on my phone to put a Bible verse up on the screen while I was sleeping, so that I physically couldn't check my phone without seeing His Word first. But gradually, before I even opened my eyes, I was looking forward to what verse would be there. I began hungering and thirsting for His Word.

I went from reading the verse, to then reading a whole chapter and lingering awhile. I prayed, I listened. I spent time with Him. I approached my entire day differently because I was filled up on truth first.

I love sitting at Jesus' feet. There is no place I'd rather be. When the things of this world tug at me, He makes known to me what is most important.

This world is noisy and screaming for our attention. But I can't even attempt to walk and live in it if I am not equipped first. Spending time with Him in His Word and prayer sets my mind and heart properly.

It's such a simple thing. Something we all should be doing without question, but so often this world drowns out what is most important. And the conversation with the Lord doesn't end once the Bible is shut and I am off and running. It is continuous throughout the day. I need Him as much as I need the air I breathe.

Read His Word first thing each day. Talk to Him first. Before you let any other voices speak into your life, let His voice be the first one you hear. Choose to set your mind on things above. Choose to sit at His feet. The joy that you will find there is like no other.

Proverbs 24:30-31

Observation	Interpretation

Application

Proverbs 24:30-31

went by the field of the lazy man,
And by the vineyard of the man devoid of
understanding;
And there it was, all overgrown with thorns;
Its surface was covered with nettles;
Its stone wall was broken down.

My Notes

Proverbs 24:30-31

My Prayer

Proverbs 24:30-31

A Note from Karen

Our garden was less than stellar this year. The weeds overtook it and pretty soon they were out of control. And as I stood in the midst of the overgrown mess I had this thought:

"We all have weeds that choke out the good fruit in our lives."

Raising my hand.

First, let's talk about the weeds. Just like those pesky little plants that grow in my garden and threaten to take over the beds if I don't pluck them daily, the sins in my life do the same.

I need to constantly keep in check those things that want to choke out the good fruit in my life. For me those sins will be different than yours.

For instance, I struggle with anxiety. Just when I think it's under control and I don't really have to check on it, worry threatens to overtake me. Like a garden bed left unchecked.

The best way to keep those sins under control is to keep the garden watered, filled with nutrient-dense soil, flooded with sunshine, and then persist in plucking the weeds that will inevitably grow.

For us, when we are well-watered with the Living Water, we are flooded with the SON, and we have His Word as our vital nutrients, we will thrive. See how God does that? Beautiful life picture right there in His Creation!

What weeds are choking out your garden? What needs to be pulled so it doesn't choke out the fruit?

Do you need to add more Living Water, the Son, and rich soil with nutrients to your life?

Today, choose to focus on tending to your spiritual garden. If not, it can be quickly overrun with weeds, and will only make it more difficult to get rid of all those things choking out the fruit and the harvest.

2 Corinthians 5:7

Observation	Interpretation

Application

2 Corinthians 5:7

For we walk by faith, not by sight.

My Notes

2 Corinthians 5:7

My Prayer

_____
_____
_____
_____
_____
_____
_____
_____
_____
_____
_____
_____
_____
_____
_____
_____
_____
_____
_____
_____
_____
_____
_____
_____
_____

2 Corinthians 5:7

A Note from Karen

So many of us are burdened daily by the need to know the outcome of things. We pray but are we really looking for a glimpse into the future to know that all will turn out our way. *And if it doesn't?*

We play scenarios in our heads over and over of the different endings to our stories or our circumstances. We try to figure it all out and line it all up. We want to know the unknown future, even when God hasn't revealed it yet.

I remember many years ago driving in some really dense fog. All of a sudden it came out of nowhere, and I couldn't see but inches in front of me. I had to go ever so slowly, barely creeping along because I had almost no visibility of what was ahead. It was really frightening, but in that moment I realized that I could only deal with what was right in front of me at the moment, inch by inch.

Just like life. Sometimes God tells us to slow down to a crawl, and since we only can see a tiny bit at a time, we must trust Him in what lies ahead. If we start go too fast we may crash. The fog doesn't allow us to get ahead of ourselves. It keeps us focused on only what is right in front of us at the moment.

God puts certain circumstances in our lives like that fog, so we can fully trust Him. We only know where we are in the present moment, because God hasn't revealed to us what is up ahead yet. It isn't time. But He wants us to trust Him. He knows what is ahead. Go slowly and trust Him.

When we try to figure out the future, we are burdened by what hasn't been revealed to us yet.

We make up scenarios, we fix our eyes on false assumptions, and we prepare for things that may never happen. But when we slow down in the moment, and know that God is only revealing what wet truly need to know, we can be assured He will bring us to safety. No matter what lies ahead. Because the truth is, if we are in His loving arms we are already safe.

Are you trying to get ahead of yourself today? Are you trying to see things you weren't meant to see yet? Are you burdened by the what-ifs?

Maybe you are being slowed down by God so that you can fully rely on Him. Walk in faith. Not by sight. Cling to Him and know that no matter what lies ahead of the fog, He is already there, holding you in the palm of His hand, safely.

Trust the outcome of your current circumstances. Don't overthink them, but walk by faith.

Psalm 119:162

Observation	Interpretation

Application

Psalm 119:162

I rejoice at Your word
As one who finds great treasure.

My Notes

Psalm 119:162

My Prayer

_____
_____
_____
_____
_____
_____
_____
_____
_____
_____
_____
_____
_____
_____
_____
_____
_____
_____
_____
_____
_____
_____
_____
_____

Psalm 119:162

A Note from Karen

Do you treasure God's Word? I mean, really treasure it? Like a precious gem? Or a valuable gift?

I remember the first time I opened the Bible and really read it. I truly felt in that moment, I had the greatest treasure in my hands that I had ever known. I couldn't get enough. The light was turned on! I just knew this book was the most precious thing I would ever own.

We treasure so many things in our lives. We lock them up, we keep them safe, we hold onto them tightly to protect them.

We treasure our technology–our phones, tablets, and laptops. We treasure our people–our families, our friends, our tribe.

We treasure our homes. We may even have security systems in place. We lock them up.

But our greatest treasure is one thing that can't be taken from us. God's Word. It is living, active, and transforming.

Treat it as such.

A treasure. More precious that *any thing* in your life. And one that can't be lost or stolen.

Treat your Bible like the treasure it is. Hold onto it more dearly than anything else you own. Praise God for it. Cherish it. Every precious word is a gift from our Loving Father.

Proverbs 13:7

Observation	Interpretation

Application

Proverbs 13:7

There is one who makes himself rich, yet has nothing; And one who makes himself poor, yet has great riches.

My Notes

Proverbs 13:7

My Prayer

Proverbs 13:7

A Note from Karen

What does it really mean to live simply?

Do you have to follow a list of rules and regulations?
Do you have to sell all your stuff?
Do you have to live on a farm?
Go off the grid?
Do you have to homeschool?
Do you need a tiny house?

NO! There are absolutely no rules and you certainly don't have to follow another person's lifestyle. The external results of a simple life focused on Jesus may mean less things, but the true focus of living simply is to get rid of anything that hinders us from our walk with God.

For me, my mission in living a simple life is because I want more Jesus and less of this world. I believe God will use people in different ways for different purposes, but all for His glory. God will lead you in how you should live, if you seek Him wholeheartedly. He may place you smack in the middle of the city or across the world, but if your focus is on Him, you will naturally seek more of Him and less pleasures of this world. I truly believe the more you desire Him, the less you will want of this world.

We are all a work in progress, so let's link arms and encourage each other in our journeys. Rather than worrying about a list of rules, let's set one rule:

Seek Jesus with all your heart. The rest will fall into place.

The direct outflow of your heart as you walk with Jesus will bring less disorder into your life that the world creates. It may mean less focus on material possessions and allowing less junk into your mind.

A simple life is the result of an uncluttered soul. There is so much joy in being filled with Jesus.

Has your life become too complicated? Are you filled up on the wrong things? Choose today to have less stuff and more Jesus. Get rid of the things that take the place of Him as first in your life.

Seek Jesus with all your heart. The rest will fall into place.

Proverbs 23:4

Observation	Interpretation

Application

Proverbs 23:4

Do not overwork to be rich;
Because of your own understanding, cease!

My Notes

Proverbs 23:4

My Prayer

_____
_____
_____
_____
_____
_____
_____
_____
_____
_____
_____
_____
_____
_____
_____
_____
_____
_____
_____
_____
_____
_____
_____
_____

Proverbs 23:4

A Note from Karen

"I'm so busy." It's our mantra these days. We are all so busy. There's never enough time. Our calendars are packed and our days are overflowing, but are our hearts?

In a culture that equates busyness with success, be free from the burden of a full schedule, with an empty heart. Be free from keeping up with Joneses. Listen to God about how you spend your time and also when you should rest.

So many of us are running around trying to keep up with the world around us. It seems these days, busyness is a badge of honor. We don't dare let a few minutes into our schedules without filling them up.

I actually shut down when I get too busy. When my days are too full I don't function well. I need lots of margin. There was a time when I wouldn't have wanted to admit that. But I am free from that now, because I know that God doesn't intend for us to be busy just for the sake of being busy.

And life isn't a competition. There are no prizes for the one who is busiest.

Yes, we should work hard. Yes, we should labor. Yes, we should be diligent. But where does it say we can't have rest? In fact, the Bible tells us we should rest.

There's something beautiful about taking downtime, especially when it refuels you so you can work again.

And what are you working for? Is your busyness bearing fruit?

I have certain seasons in my life where I am really busy, and I can handle it knowing it is a season. But also, I know I am doing what the Lord has called me to do and it is fruitful. It doesn't feel like a burden.

If your busyness feels burdensome to you, then it is time evaluate if that is how the Lord wants you to spend your time.

Why are we trying to keep up with everyone around us? We are filling up our schedules, but what about our hearts? Are they full?

Life is short. Let us be good stewards of the amount of time God has given us. Let us be busy doing things that are fruitful. Let us fill up on life-giving and God-honoring activity.

Today, take time to rest. Don't wear busyness as a badge of honor. Serve with gladness, work with diligence, and go at the pace the Lord has set before you.

Romans 12:18

Observation

Interpretation

Application

Romans 12:18

If it is possible, as much as depends on you, live peaceably with all men.

My Notes

Romans 12:18

My Prayer

_____

_____

_____

_____

_____

_____

_____

_____

_____

_____

_____

_____

_____

_____

_____

_____

_____

_____

_____

_____

_____

_____

_____

_____

_____

_____

_____

_____

Romans 12:18

A Note from Karen

The original group chat was a coffee klatch. Nowadays, though, most conversations are in an online space. And it has become one-dimensional. So much is lost in the translation without eye contact, real-life connection, and physical presence.

Technology has changed (and complicated) our relationships. We are too quick to text, email, and comment, but not reach out in real life. And things often become more complicated when we isolate or keep our distance.

I am the first to admit this an area in which I struggle. I am more comfortable writing my words in a text or an email than picking up the phone or stopping by a friend's house. But so much is lost there. Looking into someone's eyes. Hearing their voice. Feeling the touch of a hand or a hug.

Recently, I was going to spend some time writing in the local coffee shop. I was so thrilled that technology allowed me to order from my phone, walk in, grab my order, and sit down in a booth with my head behind my laptop. All the while, I didn't need to have any physical interaction with anyone. Or, I could order from a kiosk. Still, no human connection needed.

While this is convenient, if we all do this every time we order, there is much to be lost in our society.

Human interaction. Small talk. Cultural politeness. It may seem easier to order online, but when you look at it as a whole, we lose so much.

Humans were made to be in relationships. We were made for connection. When we begin to go down a path where online community takes place of physical community, we miss out on our God-given need for each other.

And when we talk via text or email, we often clutter up our lives even more because we tend to translate the words in our own tones. Disagreements often start between my husband and I because I was sure he meant a text differently than he did, all because I translated the tone incorrectly.

Or how about the numerous downright awful arguments that happen online all because we speak from behind a screen, unfiltered.

Let's get back to simple. Front porch sitting. Civil discourse. Morning pleasantries when we buy our coffee. A smile as you walk by someone. Societal niceties and manners.

Today I challenge you to simplify your life by going back to the way relationships used to be. Stop over a friend's house, meet up for lunch, or gather around the kitchen table for some good conversation. Don't let the online world clutter up your spirit. Find joy in each other. Pray together. Share together. Live lives for Christ, together.

Colossians 1:17

Observation	Interpretation

Application

Colossians 1:17

And He is before all things, and in
Him all things consist.

My Notes

Colossians 1:17

My Prayer

_____
_____
_____
_____
_____
_____
_____
_____
_____
_____
_____
_____
_____
_____
_____
_____
_____
_____
_____
_____
_____
_____
_____
_____
_____
_____
_____

Colossians 1:17

A Note from Karen

We all want control. We plan, we prepare, we make lists, we organize our homes...all good things. Yet, sometimes we go overboard.

We get wrapped up in the plans. We think if we just get the right planner, the right system in place, the perfect method, we will finally get our lives under control. And there is something to be said for order and discipline. God wants that.

Yet, God also tells us to give up control. He wants our lives surrendered to Him.

So in our quest to control our lives and every detail, we are forgetting that the Christian walk is about giving up control. He controls us.

None of our man-made systems or ordered lives will ever work if we don't grasp that truth. He is in control.

Then, from a life surrendered to Him, it really doesn't matter what method we choose, what planner (truthfully a blank notebook is just fine) or what system we implement. Because the One who orders our steps will order our lives.

We have made control an idol. We make to-do lists, goals, and plans. We focus on what we can achieve, and how we can do it, in 10 easy steps.

The Christian life is far from easy and far from a neat and orderly list.

It is often difficult and the steps don't always fall into place in perfect order.

But God.

He is working in us and through us to order our steps.

He is working in us as we surrender our lives to Him.

He is working for us as we lose control to the One who controls all things.

So I ask you today...whatever it is you are constantly trying to control...first surrender to Him. Let Him order your steps. Don't seek a false sense of control in worldly ways, but find true order, in the One who controls us. Lose control and let the One who controls all things lead you. It is the only way.

Genesis 1:26-27

Observation

Interpretation

Application

Genesis 1:26-27

Then God said, "Let Us make man in Our image, according to Our likeness; let them have dominion over the fish of the sea, over the birds of the air, and over the cattle, over all the earth and over every creeping thing that creeps on the earth." So God created man in His own image; in the image of God He created him; male and female He created them.

My Notes

Genesis 1:26-27

My Prayer

_____
_____
_____
_____
_____
_____
_____
_____
_____
_____
_____
_____
_____
_____
_____
_____
_____
_____
_____
_____
_____
_____
_____
_____
_____
_____
_____

Genesis 1:26-27

A Note from Karen

Hard work. We need it. But we avoid it. We try everything we can to make our lives easier. But in the end we sacrifice quite a bit when we take short cuts.

I spent a good part of the afternoon recently with my little "farmer boy" son cleaning out the goat pens. What a job! Phew. Not only is it smelly and gross, but it was also HARD work. I hadn't done that job before, but he sure had.

As we shoveled and made trips back and forth with the wheelbarrow, he looked over at me with a grin ear to ear and said, "I LOVE this job."

As I was knee-high in hay and goat "stuff" I wasn't so sure *that* was how I would describe my feelings at the moment, but then as I looked around...and took it all in...yes, I could say that I loved it too.

Now, I didn't enjoy the stink or scraping "stuff" off the floor, or the heavy lifting of every load into the wheelbarrow, but yes...spending time with my little one and realizing this is truly his passion. He loves these animals. He loves taking care of them. He loves hard work.

In an age of screens and a culture of self-centerdness, always choosing quick and easy...it felt good to choose hard work.

God intended us to work hard. In fact, before He the Fall, He showed us that hard work is good, because it existed in the garden before sin. God created us to work. We were created to create, to care take, to be diligent, and not lazy.

I think sometimes we make life more complicated when we take short cuts. In a world that is always trying to make things easier, it can complicate our souls. Our bodies need to move, sweat, and work. We need to feel accomplished and have work ethic. We need to have responsibility and perseverance.

Today, instead of taking the easy way, remember God created you to work. How can you glorify Him in that work?

Take time to slow down and do a task instead of rushing through it to get it done. You will connect with your Creator. God worked for six days before resting, and declared it all good. So enjoy the work He created you for.

Psalm 119:105

Observation	Interpretation

Application

Psalm 119:105

"Your word is a lamp to my feet
And a light to my path."

My Notes

Psalm 119:105

My Prayer

_____

_____

_____

_____

_____

_____

_____

_____

_____

_____

_____

_____

_____

_____

_____

_____

_____

_____

_____

_____

Psalm 119:105

A Note from Karen

Are you measuring all you do against the Word of God? Or are you sometimes walking blindly through life?

The Creator of the universe Himself speaks to us through His Word. He gives us truths to live by. We don't have to walk through life confused or lost. Yet, many of us are. We make choices without biblical discernment. We follow after the wrong people. We stray off of the right path.

Yet, all along His Word is there. It is guiding us as a lamp to our feet.

I know someone who was taking a trip. She set her GPS to the destination and started off on the drive. About forty-five minutes in, she realized things didn't look familiar and she wasn't sure she was even near her destination. When she checked the GPS, she realized she had entered the wrong address and was not anywhere near the destination. She had driven all that way in the wrong direction, and now had to back track in order to get back on the right path. All because she didn't double check the directions. She just assumed they were correct and never made sure they lined up with where she was supposed to go.

Isn't that just like us?

Do we blindly follow what someone tells us? Do we blindly follow the world's ways? Do we double check to make sure what we are following lines up with God's Word?

Often, we follow after things that lead us to the wrong places.

We are so blessed to have the Word of God as our guide and as the absolute truth in which to measure all we do. We don't have to flounder or stray. We have all we need to light our paths. His Word never fails. It is always true. And it will guide us. We just need to read it.

If we follow after the world, we may get lost and off our path. It will be a costly mistake to go back and reroute ourselves, when we could have just followed God in the first place.

Today, remember to measure everything you do, everything you hear, and everything you see against the Word of God. If it doesn't line up with His truths, it wasn't meant for you. We must use His Word as our guide in life. Not others. Not the world.

There is freedom and joy in knowing you are on the right path and not getting distracted by others. He will guide you every step of the way.

John 16:33

Observation	Interpretation

Application

John 16:33

These things I have spoken to you, that in Me
you may have peace. In the world you will have
tribulation; but be of good cheer,
I have overcome the world."

My Notes

John 16:33

My Prayer

_____
_____
_____
_____
_____
_____
_____
_____
_____
_____
_____
_____
_____
_____
_____
_____
_____
_____
_____
_____
_____
_____
_____
_____
_____

John 16:33

A Note from Karen

Peace. We all crave it. The world has never found it. Since the beginning of time wars have waged all around. And in our souls, it is the same. Battles have taken place in our minds and souls since the beginning.

But when we listen to Jesus' words and realize that this world will never give us the peace we desire, we can stop striving for it. Jesus promised trials here. That is a fact.

Half the battle is won knowing this.

Sometimes I feel like life is one of those whack-a-mole games. As soon as I put to rest one trial, another one pops up. And I get distressed. It seems that peace only lasts momentarily before another hardship is on the horizon.

But the closer I get to God and the more I walk with Him, the more I realize it isn't about getting rid of the trials for good. It is about being prepared for the next one. Because there will be a next one.

When we look at the world around us, we see battles in every area. The culture, politics, relationships. But don't despair. Those things are part of humanity here on earth until Jesus returns.

And take heed in these two comforts:

1. Jesus will return.
2. All of the trials and tribulations will end forever when He does.

In every battle here on earth, you can have peace in the midst of it. Because Jesus has overcome.

So walk through each trial with Him knowing He is in control and you are only growing closer to the Lord. No one cheerfully accepts a battle, but we can have inner peace knowing Who will win the battle in the end.

Today, no matter how much the enemy tries to steal your peace by waging battle after battle around you, look to Jesus. He is your peace right there in the midst of it.

He has overcome this world. So while we live here now, with wars waging, our peace is secure because He is victorious.

Ecclesiastes 9:9-10

Observation	Interpretation

Application

Ecclesiastes 9:9-10

Live joyfully with the wife whom you love all the days of your vain life which He has given you under the sun, all your days of vanity; for that is your portion in life, and in the labor which you perform under the sun.

Whatever your hand finds to do, do it with your might; for there is no work or device or knowledge or wisdom in the grave where you are going.

My Notes

Ecclesiastes 9:9-10

My Prayer

_____
_____
_____
_____
_____
_____
_____
_____
_____
_____
_____
_____
_____
_____
_____
_____
_____
_____
_____
_____
_____
_____
_____
_____

Ecclesiastes 9:9-10

A Note from Karen

Look around each day and you see people in a rush. They are all rushing to something, striving for something, and passing by simple moments. The hustle and bustle has become the standard.

I have always been a simple girl at heart. I have always looked at things differently as a little girl. I wondered why people always seemed to be busy, but weren't enjoying life. I never wanted my life to be lost in the hustle and bustle. I looked at things with the perspective of, "What does this matter years from now?" I always asked myself if what I was doing would have purpose.

As I grew older and had my own family, I knew I didn't want to be part of the rat race. I wanted a simple life focused on God and family. I wanted to be able to enjoy each moment. Sit in the sunshine. Enjoy creation.

Yet, the world we live in is busy. It is complicated. And early in our marriage, we were headed toward the rat race. My husband worked late hours and never was home for dinner. That wasn't a life. That was building a bank account, but not a family.

So we took a leap of faith and he began his own business. I homeschooled my kids. We wanted our family to keep up with God and not the Joneses. We moved to the country and decided to slow down and enjoy the simple.

And while I know that our lifestyle isn't for everyone, and some people enjoy the hustle and bustle, it is still important to remember who and what we are being busy for.

I ask you today–are you so busy keeping up with the world, you aren't keeping in step with God? Are you working for Him or for the hustle and bustle?

Life is so short. We must make use of our time and use it well. It isn't about just getting by, but about thriving and growing closer to the Lord.

Slow down. Enjoy the simple. And find purpose in every moment, especially the small ones. God has made you to work for Him and to live for Him. Don't let the busyness of the times distract you from what truly matters in life.

Mark 8:35

Observation	Interpretation

Application

Mark 8:35

For whoever wants to save their life will lose it,
but whoever loses their life for me and for the
gospel will save it.

My Notes

Mark 8:35

My Prayer

_____
_____
_____
_____
_____
_____
_____
_____
_____
_____
_____
_____
_____
_____
_____
_____
_____
_____
_____
_____
_____
_____
_____
_____
_____
_____
_____

Mark 8:35

A Note from Karen

What are you investing in? Are you holding onto riches or are you storing them up in eternal accounts?

In a world that tells us we need to invest for the future and save for "someday," I want to invest in the Kingdom. I want to invest in people. Relationships. Service. Jesus.

I want to invest in eternal rewards and not fleeting earthly pleasures.

I am building His Kingdom, not my own little kingdom here in my house.

What does it matter if I have a house stored up with earthly treasure, a bank account that is secure, or a neatly outlined plan for my day, but I have not invested in the Kingdom?

I don't want to sit in my comfortable bubble and make no difference for eternity. I want to get out there and live life, an adventurous life, and grab hold of every opportunity the Lord gives me.

When we share our life, we share His love. And that is an eternal investment.

Staying in my own little world and not reaching out into the world is comfortable, but is that really what God wants? He didn't give me this life to live for myself! He gave me a life to use to reach others and to glorify Him in all I do.

Sitting in my comfortable bubble doesn't bring Him glory. It is selfish on my part.

What if we use our resources for investing in things that will ultimately share Jesus? And trust Him that when we use what He provides for His glory, we have no fear of the future. He holds our life and our future in His hands!

Whenever I live in faith over fear, I know I am in God's will and the Spirit is carrying me. It is freeing not to carry myself!

So, today let go of the fear of not having enough or investing in the future (which isn't promised) and live in faith. Let God provide for your every need. Invest in others for a secure and rewarding return.

Romans 15:13

Observation

Interpretation

Application

Romans 15:13

Now may the God of hope fill you with all joy and peace in believing, that you may abound in hope by the power of the Holy Spirit.

My Notes

Romans 15:13

My Prayer

Romans 15:13

A Note from Karen

For some reason, we don't like empty spaces. We want them filled. If your home has an empty wall, it needs to be decorated. Or how about an empty shelf? Fill it up.

Or the empty time in our schedule? It makes us uncomfortable. Like we should be doing more. We feel the need to be busy and look successful in the world's eyes.

And what about empty spaces in the day where you have a minute to really breathe and sit alone with your thoughts, but you find you get uncomfortable there? So you quick grab your phone...just to check...and fill in that empty moment. A distraction seems to be more comfortable than your thoughts at the moment.

We fill and we fill and we fill. Emptiness makes us uneasy.

An empty room is not a sign of weakness. It is a sign of self-control. A moment in the day to breathe and be alone with your thoughts is a gift, not a place to escape from. An empty date on the calendar is something to be cherished, not ashamed of.

We are subconsciously told to fill, fill, fill. And the result is homes that are overflowing, minds that are cluttered, and folks that are frenzied.

How often do you fill that empty moment standing in line at the grocery store by checking your phone? What if we took notice of those around us and exchanged a pleasant, "How do you do?"

What if instead of trying to fill a moment with checking our email, we picked up the phone just to check on a friend?

Or what if instead of choosing to fill that empty time with scrolling your phone and checking to see what others say, you opened your Bible to see what He says?

Empty spaces are not uncomfortable. They are gifts. Blank slates to do with as we please...so let us use them to get closer to the Lord, and not closer to the world.

Fill your empty spaces with Him today. When you have a quiet moment, talk to Him. When you have some unexpected time, spend it with Him. Spend it with others. But don't fill it with junk just to fill it.

Our lives are cluttered because we fill them with the wrong things. Today, choose to fill your empty places with the right things. And feel the joy and freedom that result.

2 Kings 23:25

Observation	Interpretation

Application

2 Kings 23:25

Now before him there was no king like him, who
turned to the Lord with all his heart, with all his
soul, and with all his might, according to all the
Law of Moses; nor after him did any arise like him.

(to really understand this passage, please read 2 Kings 22-23)

My Notes

2 Kings 23:25

My Prayer

2 Kings 23:25

A Note from Karen

Have you ever smashed something out of anger? Thrown it across the room? Threw it down to the ground? In a moment of fury, we want to destroy something that has brought us pain.

I love the story of Josiah in 2 Kings 22-23. Here we have the king, Josiah, finding the book of the Law after it had been lost for some time. When he read the words in it, he responded. Immediately. He was so convicted by the idolatry surrounding him, he went on a rampage.

He tore down statues, smashed idols to dust, burned wooden pieces. He was indignant. He went through the city demolishing every idolatrous item he could get his hands on.

The beauty of the story is that Josiah responded to the words He read in the Book of the Law. He recognized idolatry around him and wanted to rid the city of it all. He realized the wrongdoing that was going on and did something about it.

We don't have to walk around smashing and breaking things to dust in our homes, but we can certainly respond like Josiah to the idols in our hearts.

What things are you worshiping instead of God? What things are taking first place in your life over Him? What things are taking away from you following God's standards?

Read God's Word. We are to have nothing come before God. We are to worship Him and Him alone. If there are things such as money, success, people's opinions, health, or other idols in your life, today is the day you can choose to do what Josiah did. Smash them.

Don't just put them aside or move them. Destroy them. To dust.

Respond to the Word of the Lord. Recognize the things that are hindering your walk with Him. Then clean house like Josiah did! Destroy whatever is in the way of you keeping God at the center of your life.

Ecclesiastes 3:1

Observation	Interpretation

Application

Ecclesiastes 3:1

To everything there is a season,
A time for every purpose under heaven:

My Notes

Ecclesiastes 3:1

My Prayer

_____
_____
_____
_____
_____
_____
_____
_____
_____
_____
_____
_____
_____
_____
_____
_____
_____
_____
_____
_____
_____
_____
_____
_____

Ecclesiastes 3:1

A Note from Karen

I always notice the amber glow of autumn and the golden light that it casts on the world around me. It is quite beautiful. Every year, that familiar amber glow.

Now, I really love summer and as those long summer days start coming to an end, and the sun shines for just a little shorter time each day, my heart sinks a bit. I always miss summer. It is my favorite season.

But then, that amber glow reminds me...there is always a blessing in every season. That simple beauty was not there in the summer days. It is unique to autumn.

Just like the seasons of our lives. They come and go...we yearn for the last season at times, or we yearn for a new one...yet, we forget that right there in that season, is beauty.

Each season has its own beauty and its own purpose. Perfectly orchestrated by God. Each season holds its own plan.

I remember the season of being newly married. I yearned for a baby, and quickly I was in the next season. Then all of a sudden there were several babies, and here I was with a few little ones scampering around, wondering if I would ever get a minute to myself? If my house would ever be clean again?

"Oh, it will be better when they are older..." I told myself.

Then in that great paradox of life, they suddenly are older, and we miss the little days. Those younger years seem distant now, but they are a beautiful memory. If only I had cherished it as much while living in it.

So rather than yearn for a different season, why don't we bask in the amber glow of the one we are in? The beauty that is unique to this season of life.

God made the seasons. They are purposeful, and each one full of beauty and uniqueness. Whether it is the Springtime bursting with life, the leaves of fall withering, or the snow covered ground, there is purpose.

Whatever season of life you are in, bask in it. Cherish it. Grow in it. See the blessings. Be grateful for it. Don't yearn for the past or look to the future.

Enjoy the season you are in, before the last leaf has fallen, and you miss its beauty.

Galatians 5:22-23

Observation	Interpretation

Application

Galatians 5:22-23

But the fruit of the Spirit is love, joy, peace,
longsuffering, kindness, goodness,
faithfulness, gentleness, self-control.
Against such there is no law.

My Notes

Galatians 5:22-23

My Prayer

_____
_____
_____
_____
_____
_____
_____
_____
_____
_____
_____
_____
_____
_____
_____
_____
_____
_____
_____
_____
_____
_____
_____
_____

Galatians 5:22-23

A Note from Karen

I can't stand this clutter!
I am so tired of piles of stuff! Where does it all come from?
I need a break from the online world! I wish the Internet didn't exist!
It is all too much!

Have you ever said any of these things? Many of us get really overwhelmed by all the stuff that piles up in our homes and all the stuff that piles up in our minds. Clutter is a source of stress and anxiety. But we can't seem to keep it under control. Every year we purge and purge and vow to keep it simple, and before long it creeps back in.

We can blame our home for being too small or our lack of organization. We blame the Internet that we can't stop scrolling. We blame and blame and blame.

But do we ever stop to think that clutter control is really a matter of self-control? And self-control is a fruit of the Spirit.

What we bring into our homes and our minds isn't really about the stuff itself. Often times, it can be a lack of self-control. It isn't the stuff's fault that you brought it into the house. And it isn't the Internet's fault that you wasted three hours endlessly scrolling.

Ouch. I know.

We can't blame it on the stuff. We must look inside ourselves and recognize that when we seek God first, when we desire what He desires, when we walk in the Spirit and not in the flesh, we operate with the fruits of the Spirit. Self-control is a direct result of the Spirit working in us, because we have submitted our lives to God.

The more we desire the things of God, the less we desire the things of this world, and that includes physical and mental clutter. The less stuff we allow into our homes and our hearts that isn't necessary. The less junk we allow to take away our joy.

Today I ask you to stop the endless cycle of purging clutter only to bring it back again and admit that you are not operating with the Spirit, but the flesh. And then ask God to give you self-control. Ask God to transform your mind so that you will no longer desire the things of this world but the things He offers.

It's not about moving to a deserted island where there is no Internet or shopping. It is about your desires and your control over things of the flesh.

Stuff and online clutter isn't going anywhere. Eliminating it isn't the issue, but learning to live with it in a healthy manner is.

So evaluate what needs to go in your life that is not bringing you joy. And then leave it there. Don't bring it back in. Walk in the Spirit and put to death the desires of the flesh.

Job 38:1

Observation	Interpretation

Application

Job 38:1

"Then the Lord answered Job
out of the whirlwind…"

My Notes

Job 38:1

My Prayer

_____
_____
_____
_____
_____
_____
_____
_____
_____
_____
_____
_____
_____
_____
_____
_____
_____
_____
_____
_____
_____
_____
_____
_____

Job 38:1

A Note from Karen

Sometimes, I say I surrender it all and then hope everything will be easy. But that's not true surrender. True surrender means trusting Jesus when the winds are swirling and the thunder is roaring. When I say it, I must truly mean it.

Because quite frankly there will always be battles raging. Until Jesus returns and takes us home to an eternity where He reigns forever, the battles here will still rage. And that is where surrender wins. We surrender knowing that can mean a storm may come. But Jesus is right there in the midst of it all.

The truth is, life is not defined by our circumstances but Who is in our circumstances.

God is sovereign and supreme and rules over all the earth. He rules over the storms, the still, and everything in between. So if I am going to trust Him, then I must trust Him completely. Not just when things are going my way. To trust Him *even if* a storm rages.

I remember one night I went to bed feeling extremely anxious. I laid in my bed and prayed, and just surrendered it all to God. I kept saying the name of Jesus over and over in my head. Sometimes that is all I can do to keep the negative thoughts out. *"Jesus. Jesus Jesus."* I repeated it over and over, *"I surrender it all to you."*

I fell peacefully asleep and within just a short time, was awoken by the loudest thunder I had ever heard. It literally shook the house. Followed by another monstrous sound. And another shaking of the house. And another. Then the downpour of rain. It was quite terrifying.

My phone buzzed and it was an emergency alert. It actually said, "Severe thunderstorm warning–a severe storm is spotted over (the name of my town.)"

And then I was even more scared. What about the peaceful prayers I had prayed before falling asleep, surrendering to Jesus? This is what followed? The storm is right over us!

I prayed some more. I felt the spiritual battle for my mind was being played out right outside my window. The roaring winds and rain. The beating down on my roof, the loud thunder, the bright lightning. It was far from comforting.

I couldn't sleep for hours. I prayed through it, but it was a long night.

The next morning I awoke to cool air...the kind that comes after a storm. The sun rising. The air was still outside. It was peaceful. It was quite the opposite of what went on just hours before.

I wondered why on earth did I have such a tumultuous night after praying that prayer of surrender. What was God telling me? Or was Satan really going after me?

Then it hit me, ever so peacefully.
Even in the storms. Especially in the storms. *That is true surrender.*

Today, surrender it all to God. Don't let circumstances define your joy, but let your joy come from knowing the One who is in the circumstances. Be still, even when the winds are swirling and the rain is pounding. True surrender is knowing that no matter what swirls around us, we are safe and secure.

John 12:24

Observation	Interpretation

Application

John 12:24

Most assuredly, I say to you, unless a grain of
wheat falls into the ground and dies, it remains
alone; but if it dies, it produces much grain.

My Notes

John 12:24

My Prayer

_____
_____
_____
_____
_____
_____
_____
_____
_____
_____
_____
_____
_____
_____
_____
_____
_____
_____
_____
_____
_____
_____
_____
_____
_____

John 12:24

A Note from Karen

Redemption. I love that word. I love what God does through His redeeming love. He saves us. He pulls us out of a pit of darkness and takes all that seems hopeless and replaces it with His beautiful and loving grace, peace, and hope.

One winter, during one of the most severe storms of that year, we lost a very large pine tree on our property. Thankfully there was no damage and the tree fell in an area where it was out of the way. But it sure did make a mess.

After a few weeks, my husband began to redeem that broken tree. He milled his own 18-foot wood planks and began to change our garden. He used the planks to make new raised beds for the garden and they were beautiful.

Redemption. It was all I could think about.

Taking what was once a hardship, refining it, and making it new. Something that had been destroyed was now being used for a new purpose.

The tree had to fall and die.

And those beds would now bring forth new life...literally, from those garden beds.

Just like God does in our lives all the time.

He redeems.

And look at that old wooden cross. The ultimate in redemption. What once was a rugged tree, brought life and hope to the world.

How do you see God redeeming things these days?

Today, look at life through eyes of gratitude and thank Him for redeeming your life. Even if it was painful and you had to go through trials and hardship. He makes all things new, and beautiful in His time.

Psalm 40:1-3

Observation

Interpretation

Application

Psalm 40:1-3

I waited patiently for the Lord;
And He inclined to me,
And heard my cry.
He also brought me up out of a horrible pit,
Out of the miry clay,
And set my feet upon a rock,
And established my steps.
He has put a new song in my mouth—
Praise to our God;
Many will see it and fear,
And will trust in the Lord.

My Notes

Psalm 40:1-3

My Prayer

_____
_____
_____
_____
_____
_____
_____
_____
_____
_____
_____
_____
_____
_____
_____
_____
_____
_____
_____
_____
_____
_____
_____
_____
_____

Psalm 40: 1-3

A Note from Karen

Have you been in a pit? Did God pluck you out of darkness and into His light? If so, then we should be singing His praises and telling of His glorious saving works to all who will listen. A song of praise should pour out from our mouths at all times.

He saved me straight out of a pit. Yet, there are days I get so bogged down by the things of this world, I can easily forget.

But recently I was reminded. We had two little baby ducks. They were so adorable. And those cute little baby ducks grew up to be really cute little waddling ducks that followed us around and quacked all day. They were just so endearing!

Except for one thing. They stunk.

The one thing no one tells you when you buy those adorable little ducks, is that they'll swim to their hearts content. And all the while, they will make a huge mess.

We had a little plastic pool for them to swim in and they did everything in that water–eating, drinking, and yes, pooping in it. Within minutes, that crystal clear water became a brown and muddy mess. And that mess needed to be cleaned.

So there I was one morning, dry heaving, as I sucked out that nasty water using a pump to empty it into a bucket. As I neared the bottom of the water it became really thick and muddy. And even smellier, if you can imagine that.

Yet, standing there amidst the stink to end all stink, I saw something so glorious! It was so beautiful that suddenly the stink became something to praise the Lord for! Yes, I just said that. I was praising the Lord for this muck!

You see, for years I have loved Psalm 40. Some translations use the wording, "He lifted me out of the *muck and mire*" for verse two.

And here I was, standing in the smelliest of muck and mire.

And I got it. I really got it.

He was showing me just exactly where I was before my life with Jesus. That smelly disgusting filth was exactly what life was like without Him. And you can appreciate the beauty of His saving grace even more, when you've lived in that filth.

As the years have passed, the darkness of my past has become darker the more I know Christ. But the light of the present has also become brighter. Somehow the contrast of the two work beautifully together and I see His beauty on a whole new level. And that brings praises to my lips!

May we always remember where we came from. May we not get so caught up in this world and all it offers, that we forget–God didn't leave us in the muck and mire.

Today, sing a song of praise! Don't take for granted the gift God has given you in salvation.

When you dwell on that goodness, you will no longer get distracted by this world. Sing praise!

Ecclesiastes 7:2

Observation	Interpretation

Application

Ecclesiastes 7:2

Better to go to the house of mourning, than to go
to the house of feasting. For that is the end of all
men; And the living will take it to heart

My Notes

Ecclesiastes 7:2

My Prayer

_____

_____

_____

_____

_____

_____

_____

_____

_____

_____

_____

_____

_____

_____

_____

_____

_____

_____

_____

_____

_____

_____

_____

_____

_____

Ecclesiastes 7:2

A Note from Karen

It isn't logical to think it is better to go to a house of mourning than a house of feasting, but it is true wisdom.

We spend our lives seeking more comfort and seeking more stuff, and avoiding sorrow at all costs. Rightfully, so. But the true wisdom here is the perspective.

Several years ago we suffered the loss of five different very special people in our lives in just five months. All of them were sudden. Most were young folks, leaving children behind. Every aspect of these deaths were painful. They were tragic and sudden. And it was one after the other. One funeral a month for five months. It was a time of deep sorrow.

And I remember walking out of the church at one point for the service of a dear friend, who had just left behind a widow and six children, and I thought to myself, "That's it. Life will be different now. None of the nonsense I stress over daily matters."

In that moment after being so close to death and mortality so many times, I vowed nothing mattered except knowing God and making Him known. I was well aware of my own mortality and my perspective was laser-sharp in the moment. I had an eternal perspective like never before.

Yet, as a few days passed and then weeks and months, I fell right back into the old life. Fretting about details, not focused as much as I should, less praying, less time with God.

The further I was from the tragedies, the less focused I became.

That is the wisdom in this passage. When we are in the house of mourning we are faced with mortality, we are faced with eternity, and it brings us to our knees.

But when we have plenty, times are good, and we are feasting, we can easily focus too much on the here and now. Eternity seems like something way off in the future and we don't give it much thought.

Eternity is now. We must remember that this life isn't all there is. The little details we focus on, the worry, the chasing after nonsense, the filling up on stuff…all of it…it is a distraction. When we are feasting, we are missing out on hunger for the Lord.

Today, don't wait to be in the midst of tragedy in order to regain focus. Keep an eternal perspective.

Don't let the gluttony of the world, deny you the hunger for God. Keep your eyes on what truly matters.

Deuteronomy 6:5-6

Observation	Interpretation

Application

Deuteronomy 6:5-6

You shall love the Lord your God with all your
heart, with all your soul, and with
all your strength.
"And these words which I command
you today shall be in your heart."

My Notes

Deuteronomy 6:5-6

My Prayer

_____
_____
_____
_____
_____
_____
_____
_____
_____
_____
_____
_____
_____
_____
_____
_____
_____
_____
_____
_____
_____
_____
_____
_____
_____
_____

Deuteronomy 6:5-6

A Note from Karen

So many of us are divided. We give our attention to things half-heartedly. We aren't devoted fully to many things, but often give a little bit of attention to many things all at once. We are masters of multi-tasking.

But our love and devotion for the Lord should be 100% all-in, all the time.

Wholeheartedly means undivided. There is nothing that could take our focus off our first and only love.

So loving God with our whole heart, soul, and strength means everything we do will outflow from that relationship with Him. We make choices based on our relationship with Him. We make decisions with Him at the center.

And God has commanded this of us. It should be taken seriously. Do not divide your devotion. You can't love God half-heartedly. You must be fully giving Him your all.

Imagine if you hired someone to do a job and they were showing up late, or sometimes didn't show up at all. What if they didn't really do the job well because they were tired from giving all their attention to another job?

We don't want to give God our extra time or our extra leftover anything. We don't read the Bible because we have a little spare time. We read it first because it nourishes our soul. We don't follow Him when it is convenient, but in all things, all the time.

Today, remember your first and only true Love. And give Him your whole heart, soul, and strength. A divided heart is never fully satisfied. But a heart that is fully committed, produces joy.

2 Timothy 2:21

Observation	Interpretation

Application

2 Timothy 2:21

Therefore if anyone cleanses himself from the
latter, he will be a vessel for honor, sanctified
and useful for the Master, prepared
for every good work.

My Notes

2 Timothy 2:21

My Prayer

_____
_____
_____
_____
_____
_____
_____
_____
_____
_____
_____
_____
_____
_____
_____
_____
_____
_____
_____
_____
_____
_____
_____
_____

2 Timothy 2:21

A Note from Karen

There is one question you can ask yourself everyday to change your life.

Is this honoring God?

Is what you are doing honoring God?
Is what you are saying honoring God?
Is what you are thinking honoring God?
Is how you are treating others honoring God?
Is what you are bringing into your home honoring God?
Is what you are putting before your eyes honoring God?

God doesn't exist to make you happy. You exist to glorify Him. And in everything you do or say or think, you are either honoring Him and giving Him glory, or you aren't.

Imagine if we all just asked ourselves these questions before we spoke, acted, or even had thoughts? We would move mountains in this world! We would be living as we should—all for the glory of God.

We get distracted though. We are enticed by the worldly stuff. But when we remember that our lives are not about us, but about Him, it changes everything.

Start asking yourself this question everyday. Before every thing. It will change your life as you fully follow Him.

Luke 12:15

Observation	Interpretation

Application

Luke 12:15

And He said to them, "Take heed and beware of covetousness, for one's life does not consist in the abundance of the things he possesses."

My Notes

_____
_____
_____
_____
_____
_____
_____
_____
_____
_____
_____
_____
_____
_____
_____
_____
_____
_____
_____
_____
_____
_____
_____

Luke 12:15

My Prayer

_____
_____
_____
_____
_____
_____
_____
_____
_____
_____
_____
_____
_____
_____
_____
_____
_____
_____
_____
_____
_____
_____
_____
_____
_____
_____
_____

Luke 12:15

A Note from Karen

If you are looking around now and see nothing but clutter, don't be discouraged. There is hope.

Here are some questions to ask:

Do you need it? (or more than one of it?)
Is it useful? What is the purpose for keeping it?

If you are looking around and don't even know where to begin, remind yourself to just begin with something.

If you look at the overall task it will seem overwhelming, but if you promise to get rid of one thing each day....you will be on the road to progress.

Less clutter means less to manage and more time for real things, which leads to freedom and joy.

You don't have to be a slave to your stuff. You can be free!

Picture yourself walking into a room and just enjoying it for who is in there! Don't fill spaces trying to fill voids.

Enjoy life. Real life with people, not stuff.

Several years ago, we moved to our little hobby farm in the country. We didn't use movers. We packed all we could into a 26-ft. U-Haul. It was quite surreal. Our whole life packed right there in a truck. But it was so freeing!

I didn't want to bring anything with us that we didn't really need. I wanted to live free from stuff and clutter.

Now, it doesn't mean you have to be a minimalist, but to live simply means to set your mind on what you truly need.

Clutter clouds your view. But when you get rid of the extra, you can see so much more clearly.

Evaluate today what you truly need and what is weighing you down. Choose to let go of all that hinders you and all that is a burden. Live free of clutter and find joy and freedom!

Hebrews 4:12

Observation	Interpretation

Application

Hebrews 4:12

For the word of God is living and powerful, and
sharper than any two-edged sword, piercing even
to the division of soul and spirit, and of joints
and marrow, and is a discerner of the thoughts
and intents of the heart.

My Notes

Hebrews 4:12

My Prayer

_____

_____

_____

_____

_____

_____

_____

_____

_____

_____

_____

_____

_____

_____

_____

_____

_____

_____

_____

_____

_____

_____

_____

_____

Hebrews 4:12

A Note from Karen

Everywhere we turn these days life is guaranteed to get simpler. Try this new product and it will change your life. Eat this food and you will feel great. Or do these quick simple steps and you will find happiness. We are promised more for less and we embrace it. We all want more with less work and less time. We want instant gratification. It's a fast-food mentality.

But the kicker for me are the "quick-read Bibles." Everywhere I look these days I see the same message: *"Read the Bible in just a few minutes each day"* or, *"The One-Minute Bible."* Wait, we want to read the Bible less?

No.

The Bible is the one thing in this world that we want to do more of, because the more time we spend there, the more we are transformed.

If we want to live an easier and simpler life, the truth is we need to read the Bible MORE. The more we read, the less we desire to be like the world. The more we read and connect with God, the more the desires of the world fade away, and our souls are at peace. Life gets simpler right there.

This world offers a quick fix, but the Bible is a lifelong gift.

I know the more time I spend with God, the more time I want to spend with Him. The more I read, the more I am energized. The more I listen, the more I am transformed.

Don't succumb to quick. Linger over God's word. Stay longer than you planned. It is where transformation will take place. God's Word doesn't offer the promises this world does. And there is no quick fix.

It offers so much more than you ever imagined. It is alive and powerful and will change you.

Make it a priority. Each and every day. It is not a chore, but a life-giving, life-transforming practice.

God's Word is the answer to all of our questions. Why would we want to spend just one minute or five minutes each day there?

Evaluate your time in the Word today. Choose more, not less.

Job 13:15

Observation	Interpretation

Application

Job 13:15

Though He slay me, yet will I trust Him.
Even so, I will defend my own ways before Him.

My Notes

Job 13:15

My Prayer

_____
_____
_____
_____
_____
_____
_____
_____
_____
_____
_____
_____
_____
_____
_____
_____
_____
_____
_____
_____
_____
_____
_____
_____
_____
_____
_____

Job 13:15

A Note from Karen

I used to be paralyzed by fear – fears of death or suffering or loss of loved ones. Yet, as time goes on I am realizing instead of fearing what if, I am focused on even if. Instead of focusing on what if, I focus on what is. And God is in control, even if...

Adversity is real. It comes even to the ones with the strongest faith. It comes to those with weaker faith. It doesn't pass over anyone. It is guaranteed to come.

And like Job, the reasons may not be understood, but what is understood is God is still on the throne. He is still good. Suffering doesn't change Him and who He is, but it will change us.

It will change us for good if we allow it to be used for His glory.

Life isn't for our comfort. It is for His glory. What looks hopeless is just the beginning of the endless hope and grace and love He offers.

Those things never run out. I can't fathom that! His love, grace, mercy, and hope will never run out. Suffering here on earth will end, but what He gives us, is forever.

Live less in fear of what is to come and more in faith of what has come. Jesus.

Even if this earth which gets darker everyday, fails me...He is good.
Even if the suffering here seems too immense...He is more immense.
Even if the future seems too bleak...His future is full of HOPE.
Even if life doesn't make sense...He is all we need to know.

Knowing God is more important than knowing everything. We may not understand the pain, but He heals. We may not understand trials, but He is the One who will walk through trials with us.

We can't walk around trials. We must walk through them, trusting He knows. He loves. He provides.

The Israelites– they walked through the sea...
And so will we.

Today, walk in faith, not fear, even if...because God *is*.

God is good. God is faithful. God is in control.

John 3:30

Observation	Interpretation

Application

John 3:30

He must increase, but I must decrease.

My Notes

John 3:30

My Prayer

_____
_____
_____
_____
_____
_____
_____
_____
_____
_____
_____
_____
_____
_____
_____
_____
_____
_____
_____
_____
_____

John 3:30

A Note from Karen

Sometimes I feel so out of place...

I want less, when most want more...

I want to let Him do it all, when most want to do it themselves...

I want to make it simpler, when the world is getting more complicated...

I want to live for Him, when everything shouts at me to live for yourself!

I want to put others first, even when I am told I should be first...

I want to simply live...and live simply...

...So that I can see more of Him.

How about you? Are you working toward less of you and more of Him? In everything?

In a world that focuses on the increase of stuff, the increase of ourselves, and the increase of all that is around us, let Him be our increase.

Today, choose Him over yourself. Choose to live for the purposes that He has called you.

Drown out the voices of this world so that you can hear His above all.

Let Him be your everything. Have less of what this world offers and more of what He offers. That is true gain. Forever.

Romans 12:1

Observation	Interpretation

Application

Romans 12:1

I beseech you therefore, brethren, by the mercies
of God, that you present your bodies a living
sacrifice, holy, acceptable to God, which is your
reasonable service.

My Notes

Romans 12:1

My Prayer

_____
_____
_____
_____
_____
_____
_____
_____
_____
_____
_____
_____
_____
_____
_____
_____
_____
_____
_____
_____
_____
_____
_____
_____

Romans 12:1

A Note from Karen

A Prayer for Simplicity Today

Lord, help me to put you first...
not myself, things, or even others...
but YOU alone.

Lord, help me to get rid of distractions...
remembering You alone are my hope...my peace...my eternity...

Lord, help me live more simply...so that Your ways are most clear...
and mine are not above Yours...

Lord, help me to simplify the thoughts in my mind...
so that I trust in You.

Lord, help me to cling to you from sunrise until sunset...
in all things

Lord help me to simply live...for YOU.

Today, set your mind on living for Him. It will affect every part of your day. Every word that comes from your mouth will be filtered through your desire to live for Him. Every thought in your mind will be transformed by Him. Every action that you take will be done for Him.

Colossians 3:23

Observation	Interpretation

Application

Colossians 3:23

And whatever you do, do it heartily,
as to the Lord and not to men,

My Notes

Colossians 3:23

My Prayer

Colossians 3:23

A Note from Karen

Your life has a ripple effect far beyond this moment or even your lifetime. What you do now matters well into the future and even into eternity.

My grandmother (we called her "Nanny")made us all afghans when we were little and they were intended to be given to us when we got married. Even though she had passed away before my wedding, I received mine at my bridal shower. And it has traveled with us from our first year of marriage until now.

It never ceases to amaze me that years before, many years before, Nanny sat, knitting that afghan. Never having a chance though, to see it...

wrap a pregnant mommy resting on the couch...
comfort sick kiddies in bed...
used as a roof for a fort between couch cushions...
swaddling a peacefully sleeping great-grandchild...

Nanny never even knew.

Our work here on earth stretches far beyond our years. Never underestimate something you do and how it will affect the future.

Nanny may have knitted after a day of hard work..tired...or while just passing time on a Saturday afternoon. All the while, did she ever think, as the yarn wound around her needles, where her afghan would end up? Or who it would comfort one day? Probably not.

It was probably just stitch after stitch..loop after loop...row after row...out of love.

Isn't that how life is sometimes?

We go through the motions, and don't stop and realize, everything we do can have an affect on someone else, presently, or in the future.

Today, realize that your impact matters. Don't underestimate the power of your love or your actions.

John 15:5

Observation	Interpretation

Application

John 15:5

"I am the vine, you are the branches. He who abides in Me, and I in him, bears much fruit; for without Me you can do nothing.

My Notes

_____
_____
_____
_____
_____
_____
_____
_____
_____
_____
_____
_____
_____
_____
_____
_____
_____
_____
_____
_____
_____

John 15:5

My Prayer

_____
_____
_____
_____
_____
_____
_____
_____
_____
_____
_____
_____
_____
_____
_____
_____
_____
_____
_____
_____
_____
_____
_____
_____
_____
_____
_____

John 15:5

A Note from Karen

Do you know I am a mess? Every single day. A mess. If I were to live apart from Him, it sure wouldn't be pretty.

Only by HIS power can I do anything.

When I try to do it on my own...
I yell
I complain
I am a mess
I see darkness
I am lost
I am fearful
I race

When I surrender and let His power work in me...

He quiets me
He gives me joy and contentment
I am clean
He provides the Light
He shows me the Way
He gives me faith
He stills me

I do absolutely no good thing in my own power.

That is the beauty of the Gospel. When we realize we surrender our old life for the new, His power does immeasurably more than we can imagine.

And every single day I can choose to surrender to Him and let His power work. Or try to do it on my own.

When we try to do it on our own and put our pleasures and needs first, we will always fail.

When we surrender our lives to Him, for His purposes, He is always glorified.

Can you imagine if we truly surrendered it all to Him? Imagine the power that could be unleashed in our lives to do immeasurably more than we ever imagine!

Remember today, that you can do no good thing apart from Him. So abide in Him. And watch His power work.

John 1:12

Observation	Interpretation

Application

John 1:12

But as many as received Him, to them He gave the
right to become children of God, to those who
believe in His name:

My Notes

John 1:12

My Prayer

_____

_____

_____

_____

_____

_____

_____

_____

_____

_____

_____

_____

_____

_____

_____

_____

_____

_____

_____

_____

_____

_____

_____

_____

_____

_____

John 1:12

A Note from Karen

Your clothes do not define you.
Your house does not define you.
Your friends do not define you.
Not even your family defines you.

These things help shape and mold us.

But if your house is messy...
If your house is small...
If your kids are numerous, or you have none at all...

You are not defined by our circumstances.

If your past was messy...
If your future look unsure...
If the present is unsettled...

You are still not defined by those things. We are defined by one thing alone...Christ.

And when we understand and accept the truth that His grace is enough for us, then our lives become an extension of that definition and our joy is complete in Him.

Things of this world will NEVER, EVER make us feel complete. Our circumstances and our surroundings do not define us.

We can still have joy in a mess...
Joy in uncertainty...
Joy in troubles...

Because our circumstances do not define us.

Our "stuff" of this world will not last...eternity does. Secure in Christ. Joy comes from knowing that truth. Not from a clean house, well behaved kids, or even from a spouse. Those things can bring us happiness but are not complete contentment.

By HIS grace we are saved. NOT by anything we do on our own. When we continually strive to "do good" or "do right" without FIRST accepting that His grace is enough, we will just keep running in circles trying to do right, yet still feel empty.

Today, rest in your identity as a child of God. Don't let the world define you.

Matthew 5:16

Observation	Interpretation

Application

Matthew 5:16

Let your light so shine before men, that
they may see your good works and glorify
your Father in heaven.

My Notes

Matthew 5:16

My Prayer

_____
_____
_____
_____
_____
_____
_____
_____
_____
_____
_____
_____
_____
_____
_____
_____
_____
_____
_____
_____
_____
_____
_____
_____
_____
_____

Matthew 5:16

A Note from Karen

The epitome of your home is how it looks when no one is around.

How many times I have toiled over cleaning for company. Trying to make my house look just right, so I am not judged by a messy room, a dusty table, or crumbs on the floor.

I want my home to be an inviting place, a cozy place, and a place where the love of Christ abounds.

Do I want people to come over because my house is spic and span? Or because they can relax and feel comfortable?

A house is just a house.
A home is where love flows through and is palpable in every corner.

I don't want to be fake. I want to be authentic and the truth is with four kids home all day, we get messy. I want my heart to be free from worrying about what people think of me.

I care more about doing things, than having things.

So it is my prayer to have an open home, messy or not. It is the same whether people are here or not.

Today, choose to open your home without worry. Focus on how the people in your home feel rather than impressing them with your house. A home is a haven. A house is just a shelter.

Choose to build a home, filled with the love of God. Let the light of Christ permeate every dark place in your home. No one will be able to notice the crumbs on the floor or the dust in the corner when they see Christ's love radiate in your home.

Ecclesiastes 2:4-11

Observation	Interpretation

Application

Ecclesiastes 2:4-11

I made my works great, I built myself houses, and planted myself vineyards. I made myself gardens and orchards, and I planted all kinds of fruit trees in them. I made myself water pools from which to water the growing trees of the grove. I acquired male and female servants, and had servants born in my house. Yes, I had greater possessions of herds and flocks than all who were in Jerusalem before me. I also gathered for myself silver and gold and the special treasures of kings and of the provinces. I acquired male and female singers, the delights of the sons of men, and musical instruments of all kinds.

So I became great and excelled more than all who were before me in Jerusalem. Also my wisdom remained with me.

Whatever my eyes desired I did not keep from them.
I did not withhold my heart from any pleasure,
For my heart rejoiced in all my labor;
And this was my reward from all my labor.
Then I looked on all the works that my hands had done
And on the labor in which I had toiled;
And indeed all was vanity and grasping for the wind.
There was no profit under the sun.

Ecclesiastes 2:4-11

My Prayer

_____
_____
_____
_____
_____
_____
_____
_____
_____
_____
_____
_____
_____
_____
_____
_____
_____
_____
_____
_____
_____
_____
_____

Ecclesiastes 2:4-11

A Note from Karen

We can feel the wind. We can feel it as it blows by. Yet we can not hold onto it. We can not grasp it. We can not keep it. Isn't that what we try to do though?

We chase after things of this world. The need for more stuff; the need for more busyness. Yet, that is like chasing the wind. Ultimately at the end of our life, we hold onto none of it.

What do we hold onto?
Him.

Wanting things and enjoying things in life isn't bad in and of itself. We should enjoy the fruits of our labor. But are we placing stock in those things to make us happy? Are we relying on externals with the hope that we will find satisfaction in them?

I used to feel like if I had just the right house it would make me happy. Or just the right___fill in the blank. I have come to know material things aren't that important. I enjoy my home. It is my comfort. My sanctuary. But I do not hold onto it, because ultimately I can't.

Like chasing the wind.

When you purge your life of extras and stop chasing the wind, you fix your eyes on the unseen. Ultimately, that is what you hold onto for eternity.

Fix your eyes on praying. On filling up on His Word. The more you pursue Him, the more you will want to chase Him and not the wind.

Serving God, loving people, living in His will. Today choose to stop chasing the wind and chase after Him.

James 4:14

Observation	Interpretation

Application

James 4:14

whereas you do not know what will happen
tomorrow. For what is your life? It is even a vapor
that appears for a little time and then vanishes away

My Notes

James 4:14

My Prayer

_____
_____
_____
_____
_____
_____
_____
_____
_____
_____
_____
_____
_____
_____
_____
_____
_____
_____
_____
_____
_____
_____
_____
_____
_____
_____

James 4:14

A Note from Karen

If only I had a better job...
If only I was married...
I only I could get pregnant again...
If only I had more money...
If only I lived somewhere else...
If only my kids would behave...
If only I had a better system...
If only I were more organized around here...
If only I had the latest gadget to help me...

All of us are guilty of the "if only" complex at one time or another. I know for so long I was also guilty of the "Someday when..." syndrome too.

Someday when I have kids...someday when I am married...someday when my kids are older...

We are always thinking there is more out there....down the road...that will be better.

"If only" and "someday" is not the way God wants us to live.

He has given us no more than this moment.

We are not made for this earth. We have a desire for more because inside we long for eternity. He wants us to long for eternity, not for the "somedays" of this world, because we don't know how many more somedays we have.

We must learn to be content with the here and now. Seek Him here and now. He knows our somedays and He will give us the desires of our heart when we seek Him in the here and now first.

No thing. No circumstance. No expectation can ever live up to eternity.

Live for today and don't live for someday. "If only" is just an excuse for discontent.

Choose to be content in your circumstances and know full well that someday will come, and then you will live in glory with your Savior. This world is not heaven.

So live for this moment, this day, this circumstance, and above all live for Him.

John 15:2

Observation	Interpretation

Application

John 15:2

Every branch in Me that does not bear fruit He
takes away; and every branch that bears fruit He
prunes, that it may bear more fruit.

My Notes

_____

_____

_____

_____

_____

_____

_____

_____

_____

_____

_____

_____

_____

_____

_____

_____

_____

_____

_____

_____

John 15:2

My Prayer

_____

_____

_____

_____

_____

_____

_____

_____

_____

_____

_____

_____

_____

_____

_____

_____

_____

_____

_____

_____

_____

_____

_____

_____

_____

John 15:2

A Note from Karen

Pruning things that aren't fruitful. It is a constant balance in life to maintain between what bears fruit and what needs to be pruned.

There is a nearby apple orchard that I pass by often. Every season like clockwork, the apple trees change so distinctly. In the Spring they are full with blossoms. Summer and Autumn come and they are full with beautiful ripe fruit ready to be picked. They stand there in all their glory, bursting with sweet apples.

And then when harvest time is over and the weather turns cold and gray, those apple trees stand stripped of fruit and leaves, with their branches sort of distorted and outstretched, looking naked, almost as if they are ashamed of their bareness.

The farmer has to prune them, knowing it is necessary for their fruitfulness. And Spring comes and once again those ugly bare branches, become beauties adorned with blossoms. This wouldn't happen if the farmer didn't prune back some of those branches.

I am pruning. Pruning the branches in me that are not producing fruit–the shoots that spring up and need cutting back so that the others may grow and blossom. Too much activity chokes out the fruit that could be born if there weren't so many branches begging for nourishment.

How do you maintain a balance of the fruit you are cultivating? Are you focused on a few things and doing them well, or is there only a little nourishment going to each branch?

Produce fruit of quality and not just quantity.

Sometimes, we need to take a step back in our lives, whether it be in our families, our ministry, or in our homes and assess what we are doing with our time. What we are doing with our treasure. What we are doing with our talents.

Are we bearing fruit with those things? Or are we filling up on so many things that we do not do them efficiently? Are we producing too many weeds? Are our buds beginning to blossom, but then whither from lack of nourishment?

Today, admire the Master Gardner and His handiwork. Eagerly await to see those blossoms spring forth from the ground and burst from the branches. But remember only after His careful pruning, will they bear good fruit.

Pruning is painful, but necessary. Allow Him to cut back all of the things in your life that may choke out the good fruit. Then watch as you blossom and bear the fruit you were meant to bear, all because of your Master Gardener's tender care.

Romans 8:28

Observation	Interpretation

Application

Romans 8:28

And we know that all things work together for good to those who love God, to those who are the called according to His purpose.

My Notes

Romans 8:28

My Prayer

_____

_____

_____

_____

_____

_____

_____

_____

_____

_____

_____

_____

_____

_____

_____

_____

_____

_____

_____

_____

_____

_____

_____

_____

_____

_____

_____

_____

_____

_____

Romans 8:28

A Note from Karen

"Fix it! You always do!"

Yes, I actually said these words to my husband once, after having some rather disappointing news.

Really, though my husband is the one that always works things out. I trust him completely to figure it out, work things through, and find a solution. He always does.

But this one time, even he couldn't fix it.

Sometimes that is exactly where God wants us.

Often we say we surrender to Him, but in our hearts we still cling to the outcome we desire. That's not surrender. Not true surrender.

God doesn't always want things fixed right now. In fact, in His eyes, it is already fixed. The solution is in His hands. We pray and surrender but His answer may be different from what we want. But that is the best outcome because He knows it all.

God always works things for good, even when it doesn't go our way. He always fixes it. He has far more information about everything than our little finite minds can imagine. We have just a teeny tiny amount of information about our lives. God is omniscient and literally knows every molecule of every thing in existence (which is incomprehensible to me) yet we have the audacity to disagree with Him when the outcome doesn't go our way.

How can we argue with an all-knowing God?

He promises to work all things for good, but doesn't promise it will feel good in the process. But the end result is always best. We simply can not disagree with God's outcomes. We can trust the One who holds the stars in the sky can handle our little problems here on earth. After all, I want the One who created the universe in control of my life. How could I ever want to be in control of my life? I would surely mess it up!

Sometimes, life can be difficult. It doesn't always make sense. Yet, He is weaving together every single detail just perfectly for an outcome we can't even imagine.

Today, pray with your palms up. I do this often. I open my hands of my plans and my will and surrender it all to Him. Palms up. Don't cling to your desires, but allow His desires to become your desires. Because in the end, why would you desire anything apart from His will? The One who created you knows what is best and will work all things for good.

Proverbs 19:21

Observation	Interpretation

Application

Proverbs 19:21

There are many plans in a man's heart,
Nevertheless the Lord's counsel—that will stand.

My Notes

Proverbs 19:21

My Prayer

_____
_____
_____
_____
_____
_____
_____
_____
_____
_____
_____
_____
_____
_____
_____
_____
_____
_____
_____
_____
_____
_____
_____
_____

Proverbs 19:21

A Note from Karen

I look around and see a world that is constantly trying to control itself. From schedules, to planners, to chore charts, to reward charts. To books blogs, and videos that teach how to organize. It's everywhere. We think the more "control" we have over our surroundings, the more in control we are of our lives.

The truth is, we are more in control when we surrender.

When we submit to God, and recognize that He is fully in control, and our job is to follow Him and let Him lead, we actually will find rest. We stop chasing the "better way" of doing things (in our own strength) and start chasing Him...the best way.

I am a planner addict. I've had every kind out there. At the start of a new year, when the planner is empty and ready to be written in, I get an adrenaline rush filling in all the blanks. I feel like I have control over my life!

The truth is, that blank piece of paper doesn't help me to control my circumstances. Knowing God does. Spending time with Him. Getting close to Him. Seeking Him. Then the rest of this life doesn't seem so out of control, and I don't have to spend so much time trying to organize it, just so I feel in control.

Any control that we think we have on our own, or through a system, is a false sense of control. We will only be fully in control when we are walking with Him. Then, we can move forward with our planning and our systems knowing that He is the One leading.

So I encourage you...if you have a need to control your life, let go...give it all to Him, and be at peace, knowing that you are right where you need to be. There is so much joy when you surrender to Him.

John 17:14-16

Observation	Interpretation

Application

John 17:14-16

I have given them your word, and the world has
hated them because they are not of the world,
just as I am not of the world. I do not ask that
you take them out of the world, but that you
keep them from the evil one. They are not of the
world, just as I am not of the world.

My Notes

John 17:14-16

My Prayer

John 17:14-16

A Note from Karen

Call me an underachiever, but I have always been a girl who looked at things with this perspective...

"In the grand scheme of things, what will this matter?"

I never understood putting so much time and attention into little details.

Remember the days of a regular ol' rectangle birthday cake with plain candles, or maybe the candles that tricked you and never blew out? There wasn't an elaborate theme or big fancy cake to outdo everyone else. (Kids really just want that yummy cake, and their family to celebrate with them.)

What about the days where friends gathered together and brought a covered dish, not a Pinterest-fancy recipe? Or the days where we read a handwritten note from a friend, on stationary, and it wasn't written digitally?

Ah, the simple days. The days where we could focus more on people and not things.

The world is complicated. Choose to go back to the basics. Focus on people and not details. Store up in heaven, not on earth. There is so much focus on the perfect decor, recipes, parties, outfits, you name it...but NONE of that matters in the end. It is all extra. And while it can be fun to make fancy recipes or pretty cakes or have nice outfits, sometimes it is too much.

If it takes time away from our lives, adds stress, or too much thought goes into it, we are focusing on the world. The more I see Pinterest-perfect and Instagram-ideal, the more I worry that we are moving our focus from the "grand scheme of things," to the things of this world.

This world is not all there is. Enjoy it, but do not put more time into earthly pleasures than eternal ones.

Remember that in the grand scheme of things, an elaborate birthday party will not matter. Feelings matter. Kids will remember that Mommy played with them, not that she was busy trying to make the party "just right." Or that your house was comfortable to all who entered, not that you had the fanciest decor.

It isn't always the end result that matters most, but the experience of getting there.

Today, will you join me in looking at things differently? The next time you are buried in details trying to make things "just right..." ask yourself,

"How much does this matter in the grand scheme of things?"

Simplify. Get back to the basics. Store up treasures in heaven. That is where it will matter.

Hebrews 6:19

Observation	Interpretation

Application

Hebrews 6:19

This hope we have as an anchor of the soul, both sure and steadfast, and which enters the Presence behind the veil,

My Notes

Hebrews 6:19

My Prayer

_____

_____

_____

_____

_____

_____

_____

_____

_____

_____

_____

_____

_____

_____

_____

_____

_____

_____

_____

_____

_____

_____

_____

_____

Hebrews 6:19

A Note from Karen

The pendulum is always swinging back and forth.

"I'm so organized...the house is a mess...I want routine and order....let's be spontaneous this week...I want adventure...I want to be a homebody..."

The list goes on and on. The pendulum always swaying from one direction to the other. You too?

What is it that causes these fluctuations? The constant roller coaster in life. The constant swinging motion back and forth.

We want one thing, and then shift the other way.

I know so many times I yearn for something, only to have it, and soon feel discontent again. I want order and schedules, until I feel too confined. I want freedom, until I need boundaries. I want to travel, until I feel homesick. What is going on?

Is it just our personality?
Or is it something more?

Discontent lies at the core of our souls. Look at Adam and Eve. They lived in perfection and it still wasn't enough.

We need something to ground us. To anchor us. So we can stop swinging back and forth.

When we have Jesus and we focus on what HE wants from us (not necessarily what we want) we find stability.

The pendulum swings are usually a result of our emotions and desires. But Jesus anchors us. We are stable.

The truth is the earthly life never completes us and never satisfies. We were made for eternity. We will constantly seek more or something else when our eyes are gazing downward instead of heavenward.

A life focused on God means not always relying on our emotions. It means keeping our eyes fixed on Him and what He wills for us. It may not always feel good or be easy or comfortable, but we can rest knowing we are fulfilling our purpose in Him.

So choose today to let Him balance you. Be anchored with Jesus at the center.

Ephesians 2:4-9

Observation	Interpretation

Application

Ephesians 2:4-9

But God, who is rich in mercy, because of His great love with which He loved us, even when we were dead in trespasses, made us alive together with Christ (by grace you have been saved), and raised us up together, and made us sit together in the heavenly places in Christ Jesus, that in the ages to come He might show the exceeding riches of His grace in His kindness toward us in Christ Jesus. For by grace you have been saved through faith, and that not of yourselves; it is the gift of God, not of works, lest anyone should boast.

My Notes

Ephesians 2:4-9

My Prayer

Ephesians 2:4-9

A Note from Karen

Do you ever think you need to do stuff–more stuff–to earn favor from the Lord? If you pray more, serve more, do more, He will find favor in you?

I remember when my son was very little, he was reading his little picture Bible and afterward he said, "Now what should I do, Mommy?"
"Pray." I answered. "Talk to God..."
"What should I talk about?" he asked.
"Just talk to Him. Thank Him for creating you. Thank Him for loving us. Ask Him to help you obey today."

He sat there very still, in deep in conversation with the Lord, as deep as a five-year-old can get.

Then he sat up, removed his band-aid that had been covering his big toe and said, "Look! My cut is getting better. God healed it. I did something for Him, and now He did something for me."

Oh, NO! I quickly responded we don't have to do ANYTHING to earn anything from God. In fact we can not. I wanted to make this so clear in his little mind, that he knew we never, ever do anything to get anything from God.

I went on to explain that God made us, and all we need to do is love Him back and obey. We respond to Him and do things out of love, not obligation. We don't do things in order to get things from Him. We simply love Him.

That day I realized how we all are like that sometimes. Even though we know in our heart of hearts we do nothing to earn God's favor, He freely gives us His gift of the Holy Spirit, we still try to earn it.

Nothing we ever do will earn God's love. He doesn't ask us to earn it. That is the beauty of His grace. It is a gift.

I deserve nothing from Him. In fact, what I do deserve is far worse. I have sinned so much, fallen so short, and day after day I fail. Yet, He chose to come and swoop me up from the life I was living and let me live in His grace. So instead of trying to earn anything, or even repay Him, I will give glory to Him for what He has done.

Today, accept the gift of grace. Stop trying to earn it, stop striving, and rest in Him. Your obedience is a response to His love. Meditate on that truth, and know you have been saved by grace, and not by anything you have done or will do.

John 3:16

Observation	Interpretation

Application

John 3:16

For God so loved the world that He gave His only begotten Son, that whoever believes in Him should not perish but have everlasting life.

My Notes

My Prayer

John 3:16

A Note from Karen

Life is complicated. But thankfully, Jesus is not. The truth is so simple. He is right there ready to redeem it all.

We are all running this crazy race called life, with our eyes on so many things, and our feet running in different directions. There are emotions and jobs and families and sickness, and stuff...so much stuff.

The most important truth we need to know in order to handle those things, is right here. The answers we need are so close. Yet, we strive, and we work, and we try to fix things.

It is so much simpler if we just stop. Hear the truth and be free. So free. Oh, so, free.

Life is hard and busy and full of complicated situations. Yet, He gives us such a simple message.

The beauty of the gospel is this: We don't have to do a single thing to earn salvation. In fact, we can not. It is impossible. Jesus saves. Jesus redeems. Jesus changes everything. Jesus is enough.

We don't have to strive. We don't have to earn it, or work for it, or buy it, or anything else. No earthly thing can ever rule over Him. He is enough. Jesus paid the price for us all, so our sins can be covered and we can live in heaven. That is the simple truth. We accept it, repent of our sins, and we are free. Free from any rules and legalism or any other falsehood that tells us we must do something in order to earn salvation.

The simple truth is Jesus earned it for us. We reap the reward for what HE did. Does that blow your mind? It should.

And if it does, then, and only then, do we obey, not out of guilt or to be rewarded, but out of love. Pure love. Love that should spill out of our pores into every crevice of our lives and flow into other lives, until we are spreading His love wherever we go. Love that grows because we can't get over the fact that He died for us. And we will live. We don't deserve it, yet here we are. Face to face with the truth. The beautiful truth.

So take your eyes off the world for a bit, because the truth is this world is fading and it's fading fast. The only thing eternal is Him. Take your eyes off the stuff, the busyness, the clutter, the complications, the work, the details of life...whatever it is that is keeping you from staring truth in the face. Come face to face with truth. Believe it. Be free.

So simple. Amidst the complications of life, cling to the most simple but important truth.

Jesus is enough.

Yes, today, know that Jesus is enough.

Ephesians 4:22-24

Observation

Interpretation

Application

Ephesians 4:22-24

that you put off, concerning your former
conduct, the old man which grows corrupt
according to the deceitful lusts, and be renewed
in the spirit of your mind, and that you put on
the new man which was created according to God,
in true righteousness and holiness.

My Notes

Ephesians 4:22-24

My Prayer

_____
_____
_____
_____
_____
_____
_____
_____
_____
_____
_____
_____
_____
_____
_____
_____
_____
_____
_____
_____
_____
_____
_____

Ephesians 4:22-24

A Note from Karen

Part of my desire to simplify has always been to have less stuff to manage and more time for things that matter.

Over the years, I saw that I was a manager of piles. I was a manager of stuff. I was always looking for a more efficient way to manage toys, kitchen counters, homeschool supplies, gadgets, and more. Yet the simplest solution of all has really been, just have LESS stuff.

Really. When we moved into our home, it was all new and empty. You could literally feel the weight and burden of stuff lifted.

I enjoy a level of freedom that comes from just having less stuff on a daily basis. I also work to respect our home and teach my children the same. God has provided a blessing to us, and we are to be good stewards of that blessing. We are to respect it, by keeping it clean and part of that is keeping it clutter-free.

There truly is more time to just enjoy each other, enjoy friends, and build relationships.

I have enjoyed filling my home with people. We fill it to the brim with people as often as we can. We have prayer groups, Bible studies, and just plain fun with friends. Filling up each room with fellowship and laughter makes my heart full and makes me feel like there is purpose in our home.

Our society has become quite the collectors. In fact, we have so much we need to rent storage facilities to hold all of our stuff. It boggles my mind. How is that possible?

We spend hours and hours to accumulate stuff and to organize it, yet we are never really content. Why is that?

Less stuff also gives you more clarity to see the things that remain and truly matter.

So ask yourself today, what are you filling your home with? Where are you storing your treasure? And what exactly do you treasure most? People or things? Do you have clutter or purpose?

Are you feeling anxious because there are endless piles? Then just do something today. Set out to purge the things that are weighing you down. Choose to have less, and do more...choose to simply live, for Him.

1 Peter 2:2-3

Observation

Interpretation

Application

1 Peter 2:2-3

as newborn babes, desire the pure milk of the word, that you may grow thereby, if indeed you have tasted that the Lord is gracious.

My Notes

1 Peter 2:2-3

My Prayer

_____
_____
_____
_____
_____
_____
_____
_____
_____
_____
_____
_____
_____
_____
_____
_____
_____
_____
_____
_____
_____
_____
_____
_____
_____

1 Peter 2:2-3

A Note from Karen

The other night I was well aware of this yummy peanut butter cup ice cream that was in my freezer. I couldn't wait to have some. I thought about it after dinner, and all the way until I finally pulled it out of the freezer a few hours later. YES. It was finally in my bowl and ready for me to enjoy. And I did. It was oh, so good...after all that waiting and desiring...I indulged.

As I ate that ice cream, I thought to myself, "What if I hungered for His Word as much as I did for this ice cream?"

Really.

There I was with a mouthful of peanut butter cup indulgence, convicted. I literally craved the ice cream for the whole day. Desired it. Indulged. And I was convicted. Had I desired Him as much that day?

Do we go after His Word with that kind of craving? Do we hunger for it and thirst for it as if our lives depend on it?

God's Word is transforming. I desire it more each and every day. Yet it doesn't transform me by sitting on a shelf and looking at it as I walk by. It doesn't permeate my soul unless I open it.

And then the desire comes. I hunger and I thirst for His Word and His truths. It is my spiritual nourishment.

I have been so transformed personally by His Word. Admittedly, there are days when I am convicted because I desire worldly things (such as ice cream) more than His Word. May it not always be so. May I always seek Him above all. May I always know the power of His Word. May I hunger and thirst so much for Him, that He is on my mind unceasingly – and I know my only satisfaction comes from Him.

Earthly desires and pleasures are fleeting but the soul that is filled with His Word is satisfied.

What are you hungering for these days? What importance are you putting on His Word? Is it something you do when you feel like it, or are you craving it?

We must be craving His Word and His righteousness! Let us all be so hungry we can never get enough of Him, yet we will have an eternity to satisfy our every desire.

Today, hunger for His Word, and find the satisfaction only He can give.

Isaiah 55:8-9

Observation	Interpretation

Application

Isaiah 55:8-9

"For My thoughts are not your thoughts,
Nor are your ways My ways," says the Lord.
"For as the heavens are higher than the earth,
So are My ways higher than your ways,
And My thoughts than your thoughts.

My Notes

Isaiah 55:8-9

My Prayer

Isaiah 55:8-9

A Note from Karen

Are you waiting on God to open a door that has remained closed for some time? Do you trust that God will open that door if it is best for you? Or do you get impatient and beg for it to be opened?

We have chickens and when we are able, we let them outside through their little chicken door so they can roam free, and boy do they love it. But lately, there have been hawks and foxes and we just can't let them roam free all the time. Often, the door remains closed.

Today I watched them all lining up at the door hoping I would let them out, yet I had just seen a hawk circling above. So there was no way I was going to open that door. And it dawned on me that those poor chickens just don't understand. They don't understand that I am keeping them safe from potential danger. They just want to get out and be free! They have no idea what I am protecting them from.

I realized I will never, ever, be able to explain that to them either. After all, they are chickens. I can't communicate to them just what I am protecting them from. I have infinite more knowledge and understanding than they do. They will never, ever understand, but I know day after day they will continue to stand at that door hoping I will open it.

Aren't we just like those chickens with God? Sometimes we stand and wait for Him to open a particular door, and He never does. And you know what? We may never know in this lifetime why not, or just what He is protecting us from. And He may never be able to explain it to us or make us understand His infinite and His far superior wisdom in this lifetime.

Just like I can't explain it to those chickens.

Are you standing daily at a door that God isn't opening? Perhaps He is protecting you from something or He just knows better and has a greater plan. We can't always understand and that is okay. We don't have to. Just like I have those chickens' well-being in mind, God always has our best interest in mind. He is not trying to harm us or keep us from good.

What we think we are missing out on, may very well be His loving protection.

I joke about how much I adore my chickens, but really, in all seriousness, it is amazing how much I can learn from a simple afternoon of watching those creatures...and thinking about our God and His care for us.

Today, take a lesson from those chickens. Remember that God will open and close doors for our good. He has all of the information about what is best for us and He knows far more than we do about what is on the other side. If He chooses to keep it closed, praise Him anyway.

Isaiah 40:31

Observation	Interpretation

Application

Isaiah 40:31

But those who wait on the Lord Shall renew their
strength; They shall mount up with wings like
eagles, They shall run and not be weary, They
shall walk and not faint.

My Notes

Isaiah 40:31

My Prayer

_____
_____
_____
_____
_____
_____
_____
_____
_____
_____
_____
_____
_____
_____
_____
_____
_____
_____
_____
_____
_____
_____
_____
_____
_____
_____
_____
_____
_____
_____
_____

Isaiah 40:31

A Note from Karen

It seems that nowadays when someone asks us how we are doing, the usual reply is, "Oh, just hanging in there."

It's our mantra. It's what we do. We hang in there.

The days fly by, the routine becomes mundane, the chaos seems to grow. The children exhaust us. Life exhausts us. And we hang in there. Sometimes by a thread.

Yet, Jesus doesn't want us to just hang in there. He wants us to soar. Those who hope in the Lord, RENEW their strength. They are not weary.

So why are we all walking around weary? Run down. Just hanging in. Because we are doing it by our own strength. We put our hope in ourselves, and not in Him.

Yes, I know you have an infant that doesn't sleep. Or your life is overwhelming. Or your disobedient child is giving you a run for your money. Your husband is not on board. The bills aren't getting paid. The dishes pile up and the laundry is out of control. And you just want a nap. A really long nap. I've been there. I know.

Yet, where is Jesus in all of that? He doesn't want us living day in and day out just existing. He wants us SOARING.

And there are certainly seasons of our lives when all we can do is hang in there. But we are not meant to stay there. Day after day.

I know you want to tell me that I have no idea how hard it is...that you can only just hang in there. I know. That's what I would say too...

But then I remember that everything I am complaining about and striving for, and tiring myself over: Jesus already hung on a cross for me.

And because of that, I have every reason to be filled with joy, peace, and renewed strength.

So, let's stop just hanging in there. Let's remember that Jesus came to give us life and give it abundantly!

Life is short. It goes by fast. I don't want to look back when the sun sets on my life and say, "Well, I hung in each day. I just barely made it."

I want to say, "I lived my life for Jesus! It was glorious! It was tough, but He gave me strength! I lived abundantly and with joy!"

Today, choose to stop just hanging in there and soar like the eagle.

Galatians 5:17

Observation	Interpretation

Application

Galatians 5:17

For the flesh lusts against the Spirit, and the
Spirit against the flesh; and these are contrary
to one another, so that you do not
do the things that you wish.

My Notes

Galatians 5:17

My Prayer

_____
_____
_____
_____
_____
_____
_____
_____
_____
_____
_____
_____
_____
_____
_____
_____
_____
_____
_____
_____
_____
_____
_____
_____
_____
_____
_____
_____
_____
_____
_____

Galatians 5:17

A Note from Karen

Stop window shopping for a better life.

The Internet has brought about such an abundance of information these days. And while it can be a huge blessing to have access to so much right at our fingertips, it can also lead to serious discontent, not to mention wasted time. We spend hours upon hours scrolling. Whether we are looking for things for our home, reading articles, comparing products, or just reading about other people's lives, we need to evaluate where we spend our time.

Are we spending our time window shopping for our life, or are we living it?

The allure of the Internet is that we can see it all right in front of us. We find things that we want. Even things we never wanted become our desire. Our minds are inundated with images that show us how to have it better.

We read articles about how other people do things and we covet that for our own life. We start to compare. It is a slippery slope.

We are essentially filling up our minds with how we want our life to be, yet the irony is, we aren't living the life right in front of us.

We scroll endlessly, while life passes by in the background.

Our families need us in the present. There is more contentment and fulfillment in our own real life, rather than just reading about other people's lives, or about the next best thing that promises to make life better.

Today, choose to spend your time in His Word. There and only there are the true answers to contentment, a better life, and fulfillment. Let your kids see you in the Word searching for answers rather than on the Internet scrolling by searching for answers.

Life is too short to be wasted window shopping. Live real life and live it right now.

Philippians 3:20-21

Observation

Interpretation

Application

Philippians 3:20-21

For our citizenship is in heaven, from which
we also eagerly wait for the Savior, the Lord
Jesus Christ, who will transform our lowly body
that it may be conformed to His glorious body,
according to the working by which He is able even
to subdue all things to Himself.

My Notes

Philippians 3:20-21

My Prayer

Philippians 3:20-21
A Note from Karen

Do you fear the future? Do you fear the end of this earthly life? Many of us don't think about eternity because it paralyzes us with fear. We fear the unknown or leaving our earthly lives behind.

We used to have adorable little ducklings. They started out living in our garage in a plastic tub because they weren't ready for the outdoors. But when we finally gave them a taste of life outside the garage, they were quite excited...waddling about in the grass and exploring. Quacking away..it was adorable!

You see up until that point those ducks had known no other world except a confined plastic tub in a garage with a red light shining down on them. Only once we brought them outside did they discover there is really an entirely different (and so much more beautiful) world out there! Up until then, they had no idea what existed beyond that garage.

And you know what? That is what it is like for us here on earth. There is a whole new world waiting for us someday that is heaven. We live on this earth thinking this is it, and we are content with that. And we enjoy it enough that we are afraid of leaving it.

But imagine those ducks had never left the garage? Sure, they were content in there because it was all they knew! They had no idea about grass, and bugs, and sunshine and flowers...they were content in their little plastic tub.

Are we content in the garage?

We need to have no fear about leaving this earth some day because God has a place prepared for us that is beyond our imagination...it is far more beautiful than anything we have here. And if we never left this earth, just like those ducks leaving the garage...we would never know about it. Death doesn't have to be scary when we know that there are far better things ahead.

I know it isn't pleasant to think about our earthly life being over, but the truth is, if we believe what God says, *really* believe it, we will anticipate what is to come. Not in fear, but in hope!

I am content with my earthly life, but I know without a doubt that heaven's glory is nothing compared to this garage of an earth we live in.

Today, take time to focus on eternity. It will help you make sense of what truly matters here on earth. And anticipate what is to come, with hope and joy, not fear. Don't try to distract yourself from the truth, but embrace it. Your life here will make more sense as you live with an eye on eternity.

1 Corinthians 13:12

Observation	Interpretation

Application

1 Corinthians 13:12

For now we see in a mirror, dimly, but then face to face. Now I know in part, but then I shall know fully just as I also am known.

My Notes

1 Corinthians 13:12

My Prayer

1 Corinthians 13:12

A Note from Karen

In a supercharged world, it is refreshing to unplug sometimes. To just take time to be still and quiet.

There is a saying that once in a while, all you need to do is unplug something that isn't working, plug it back in, and it will work again. It is so true, even for us!

I remember one time I went to get onto the Internet and the WiFi wasn't working. I tried the usual fixes to work out the problem, but I just kept getting error messages.

So I went for the sure fire way to fix it: I turned the WiFi off and then turned it back on again.

Voila! It worked. Sometimes technology is a little simpler than we realize. All the fixes I tried and it was as simple as turning it off and restarting it again.

Aren't we just like that? We can all use a little rebooting sometimes. Sometimes we just need to take time away from it all to really see life more clearly. To step away from the noise, the clutter, the distractions....whatever may be hindering you.

We need to seek the Lord in a quiet place of rest and peace. A little time to truly listen without all of the noise of this world. To just unplug and recharge.

Women are so busy these days, whether it is working, mothering, homemaking, grandmothering, learning as a student...no matter what stage of life, we all need to stop and remember what we are living for and Whom we are living for!

We need to step back and take our eyes off of this world and simply direct our gaze toward Him.

I love the hymn *Turn Your Eyes Upon Jesus:*

"Turn your eyes upon Jesus,
Look full in His wonderful face,
And the things of earth will grow strangely dim,
In the light of His glory and grace."

When you turn your gaze away from the things of the here and now and look to Jesus, He illuminates what truly matters. And most of the things here will be in the shadows.

This life can be so noisy and distracting. Today, choose to turn your eyes to Jesus. Look to Him when you get overwhelmed, and the things of this earth just may seem less and less pressing, as you gaze into His glorious face.

1 John 1:5

Observation	Interpretation

Application

1 John 1:5

This is the message which we have heard from Him and declare to you, that God is light and in Him is no darkness at all.

My Notes

My Prayer

_____
_____
_____
_____
_____
_____
_____
_____
_____
_____
_____
_____
_____
_____
_____
_____
_____
_____
_____
_____
_____
_____
_____
_____
_____
_____

1 John 1:5

A Note from Karen

Do you feel like many days are dark and dreary? Are you wondering when you will see the light again? Be encouraged and know the light never went out.

I remember traveling a few years back and it was so dark and foggy upon liftoff of my flight. Everything was dreary. Yet as we soared above those clouds, all of a sudden it was bright and blue, and the sun was rising there above the clouds! The light was SO bright. The colors were magnificent. I had never seen such a contrast before. From dark and gloomy to light and brilliant sunshine in seconds. It was hard to believe that the sun was there the whole time. We just hadn't seen it because we were below the clouds.

But the sun is always shining above the clouds. What a thought!

Sometimes all we see is the dark and dreary. We wonder if the sun will ever shine again in our life. Circumstances are hard. Moments are a struggle. Seasons are painful. We can't see past them.

Yet it isn't about waiting for them to pass. Because the sun is ALWAYS shining above the clouds. God is still there. Sometimes we may forget because our circumstances have clouded our view.

But the sun always shines.

God can only radiate light and in Him there is no darkness at all. But in this world we do have dark days, dark moments, and dark seasons because we are not in heaven. We are in a broken world with pain and suffering.

But God promises that when we are with Him someday His light will never stop shining. In fact, we won't even need the sun! He will be our light forever. Imagine, no more pain, no more tears, and no more dark days. An eternal light of joy and peace.

His Light is always there even if our world is dark. Today, cling to that truth. Remember on your darkest day, His Light is still shining.

Psalm 119:18

Observation

Interpretation

Application

Psalm 119:18

Open my eyes, that I may see
Wondrous things from your law.

My Notes

Psalm 119:18

My Prayer

_____

_____

_____

_____

_____

_____

_____

_____

_____

_____

_____

_____

_____

_____

_____

_____

_____

_____

_____

_____

_____

_____

_____

_____

Psalm 119:18

A Note from Karen

Do you see clearly? Or are things sometimes fuzzy?

Recently I had an eye exam because my reading glasses weren't really helping that much anymore. I noticed that things looked fuzzier when I was reading or if I was using the computer. The eye doctor said it was the usual vision changes that come from aging (sigh) and wrote me a prescription for stronger lenses.

I noticed when she was doing the eye exam just how blurry things had been. First, she examined me using my current prescription and then added a different lens.

"How's that?" she asked.

Suddenly, everything was so much clearer. I hadn't realized just how bad the problem was until she added those new lenses.

Our life is just like that. We sort of get used to the daily living and don't realize how much we aren't seeing clearly, until it gets bad enough for us to question it.

When we start to get rid of distractions in our life, whether it is physical or mental clutter, we start to see so much more clearly. Our vision becomes sharper. All of a sudden we can focus again–on things that matter.

The Bible is like those prescription lenses. When I look through the lens of Jesus, everything changes. What I thought was clear, really wasn't. It becomes so much clearer when I fill my mind with His Word! When I look at everything through the lens of the Bible, the rest of the world and the things I thought were so important, sort of fade into the background.

And Jesus becomes my focus.

Oh, to know that truth and hold tightly to it. The more we look to Him, the less we seek after the things of this world.

That is my purpose in living a more simple life. It is not merely just to live with less, but it is to live with more Jesus.

Today, will you join me on this journey to seek Him wholeheartedly? To live more simply, so we can clearly see? To let Him fill our every need. To find contentment in Him alone.

Look at life through the lens of His Word. See clearly, and more focused than ever before.

John 17:17

Observation	Interpretation

Application

John 17:17

Sanctify them by Your truth.
Your word is truth.

My Notes

John 17:17

My Prayer

_____
_____
_____
_____
_____
_____
_____
_____
_____
_____
_____
_____
_____
_____
_____
_____
_____
_____
_____
_____
_____
_____
_____
_____
_____
_____
_____

John 17:17

A Note from Karen

You know the feeling we all have when we get something new? Maybe we waited for it for awhile. Maybe it was an impulse buy. Or maybe it was a guilty pleasure. Regardless, there is the excitement and initial delight when we get something new.

But like all things in this world, the newness soon wears off, and the novelty of the thing fades away, and that new thing becomes just another thing. Eventually, even an old thing.

The excitement is gone and most likely replaced with something else. A new desire. A new want.

The beauty of this is, that although every single thing we see on this earth is temporal and will fade away, *we* will not. God declares us new creations, yet instead of wearing down and fading away like those new shiny objects, we are becoming sanctified and holy and working toward something even better. Our bodies are wearing away but we are new and becoming better as we pursue holiness.

Oh, the comfort in knowing that we will not wear away, we will not wither, we will not die! We are growing toward a new life that God himself has provided for us.

When He made us new creations, we were completely reborn. Our old selves were torn down, not just prettied up or fixed. But completely and utterly transformed and changed! We do not have to live as the old, but as a new creation in Christ. The one that is free and the one that will exist for eternity.

Oh, what a beautiful thought! May we rest in the fact that as the life we see around us is broken, wearing out daily, and full of trials, we are reborn and being molded into the image of Christ in all things. Every sorrow, every joy, and everything in between is part of the process of sanctification.

Today, focus on the fact that everything we see is degrading, but all we have in Christ is lasting and eternal. It is new and glorious. So even when it feels hard, know that you are being made holy, set apart by God, for a purpose for Him.

Proverbs 19:2

Observation

Interpretation

Application

Proverbs 19:2

...And he sins who hastens with his feet.

My Notes

_____

_____

_____

_____

_____

_____

_____

_____

_____

_____

_____

_____

_____

_____

_____

_____

_____

_____

_____

_____

_____

_____

_____

Proverbs 19:2

My Prayer

_____

_____

_____

_____

_____

_____

_____

_____

_____

_____

_____

_____

_____

_____

_____

_____

_____

_____

_____

_____

_____

_____

_____

_____

_____

_____

Proverbs 19:2

A Note from Karen

I'm a Little House on the Prairie girl at heart. Ma is my role model. I love dreaming of a slower simpler life. A pace that isn't rushed and full of hustle and bustle.

Do you find yourself rushing through your days and weeks and before you know it, you wonder how you even got here? Time seems to move at lightning speed, because we are all moving at lighting speed.

I love my coffee. I can't help myself. I love it. A few years back when the Keurig came out, it was my new best friend. A yummy cup of coffee in just seconds? Yes!

But recently, I wanted to use my percolator again. As I sat waiting for that yummy coffee to perk, it actually felt so good to wait. Wait, what? Did I just say it felt good to wait?

In our day and age, who wants to wait? We are taught to do things as quickly as possible, to make things instantaneously, and to rush to the next thing.

But here I was waiting. It slowed me down. It gave me perspective.

Yup. All while waiting for a cup of coffee.

I thought about how it was sort of nice to slowly perk the coffee. To anticipate that nice afternoon cup of coffee and to sort of get back to the basics. (I may have had a "Ma" moment!)

Sometimes the hustle and bustle of our world has become so normal we forget, it really isn't normal.

And in the waiting is where we find the blessing. We anticipate, we ponder, we find time to think. We linger. We experience the moment without rushing through it.

It's okay to wait.

A simple cup of afternoon coffee, brewed the old fashioned way. It made me stop and slow down. It made me think back to when this was the normal way to make a cup of coffee. It made me realize faster or new and improved isn't always better. When I have a friend over now, instead of handing them that little plastic pod, I'll offer them to sit a bit and wait with me for that slow-brewed cup of coffee. As we slow down, enjoy the simple, and linger in the moment.

Today, will you join me? Find one thing to do slowly on purpose. Take the time to savor something. Take the time to be still in the waiting. Take the time to remember what truly matters most. Because most of things we are rushing to really just add more stress.

God wants us to savor our time in the Word, not rush through it. He wants us to delight in Him. And delight in our moments. So take them slowly. You never know what you will find in the slow and simple moments.

Matthew 5:14-16

Observation	Interpretation

Application

Matthew 5:14-16

"You are the light of the world. A city that is set on
a hill cannot be hidden. Nor do they light a lamp
and put it under a basket, but on a lampstand, and
it gives light to all who are in the house. Let your
light so shine before men, that they may see your
good works and glorify your Father in heaven.

My Notes

Matthew 5:14-16

My Prayer

Matthew 5:14-16

A Note from Karen

Never underestimate one small act that you make. One small smile. One small gesture. One person that you tell about Jesus.

The girl who introduced me to Jesus will never know the impact she has made around the world. Unless, by divine chance (and I am holding out for that still) we meet again on this side of heaven, she will not know until we see each other in glory, the ripple effect she had!

She has no idea the impact she made, not just on my life, but on countless others. Because she told me about Jesus, I surrendered my life to Him. And in turn, I have told my children (who will carry the message to the next generation) as well as so many others through my ministry.

I imagine she never thought about that when she read the Bible to me and explained to me that Jesus died on the cross for us. I imagine she never realized the impact mostly because she was too busy sharing her immense love for her Savior. She radiated His love in everything she did. She didn't have to try. It just poured out of her, naturally.

Do you think about your impact? Tell others. Tell someone. Love others. Love someone. You never know the ripple effect it will have.

We are commanded to go and tell, and when our lives are surrendered to Him, nothing will contain us! We want to share what He has done. We can't help ourselves.

Today, don't hoard the Good News of Jesus for yourself. Choose to love others enough to tell them of His great love for them. Choose to tell one person. That one person can trickle down to countless more through generations to come. Isn't that amazing!

Let your light shine. Let His light shine. Don't hide it. Don't hoard it. Give it away freely.

Romans 12:15

Observation	Interpretation

Application

Romans 12:15

Rejoice with those who rejoice, and
weep with those who weep.

My Notes

Romans 12:15

My Prayer

_____
_____
_____
_____
_____
_____
_____
_____
_____
_____
_____
_____
_____
_____
_____
_____
_____
_____
_____
_____
_____
_____
_____
_____
_____

Romans 12:15

A Note from Karen

Drama causes clutter and hinders our walk with the Lord. And I am not talking about theater. I am talking about women and their relationships.

Unfortunately, women can often be the most dramatic. We get easily caught up in words that don't edify, words said behind closed doors, envious spirits, covetousness, and strife.

So much of our mental load can get burdened with these unnecessary behaviors.

Imagine if we all lifted instead of dragged down or healed instead of hurt? What if we celebrated each other instead of secretly being jealous? What if we ended the bitterness and strife and walked as sisters are intended to walk?

God created us for community and that community is built on the love of God. In the world, women can be catty and drama-filled. But we are not women of the world. We are women following Jesus.

Imagine the mountains we could move if we did that? The culture would notice us. Better yet, they would notice us and see Jesus in us.

Relationship weren't meant to be so messy. God created us to walk together, linking arms, sharing in joys and sorrows. We are to rejoice with others when they succeed and cry with others when they have sorrows.

Lessen your mental clutter by keeping God at the center of your relationships. A friendship built on godly principles will flourish.

Put aside grievances and choose today to be the friend God created you to be. Pray with your friends, hold each other accountable, walk together. Honor God in your friendships. This is pleasing to the Lord.

The world has enough dramatic women. Today choose to let Jesus be the center of your friendships with other women. Imagine the power that would be unleashed through us if we walked in the Spirit together as sisters in Christ?

James 1:2-3

Observation	Interpretation

Application

James 1:2-3

My brethren, count it all joy when you fall into various trials, knowing that the testing of your faith produces patience.

My Notes

James 1:2-3

My Prayer

_____
_____
_____
_____
_____
_____
_____
_____
_____
_____
_____
_____
_____
_____
_____
_____
_____
_____
_____
_____
_____
_____
_____
_____
_____
_____
_____
_____

James 1:2-3

A Note from Karen

You can't understand peace until you have had turmoil...
You can't understand joy until you have had pain...
You can't understand contentment until you have had want...
You can't understand hope until you have experienced despair...

If you have ever exercised your muscles you know the next day there is pain. Your arms are sore, your legs hurt, and it takes everything out of you to move. That is because in order for muscle to grow, it has to be a bit damaged first. You create microscopic tears in your muscles when you push them too hard, and while you rest, they grow back. But then they grow back bigger and stronger. And through this process there is always pain.

Just like our spiritual muscles. We must endure pain sometimes in order to grow. We must experience things being torn in order to be repaired. And to grow back stronger.

No one embraces hardship or sorrow, but James tells us to count it all as joy! How can that be?

I will never forget when my husband lost his job many years ago and we were devastated. An older woman at my Bible study sent me an email and she wrote,

"I know this sounds crazy, but I am so excited for you! This means God is going to be working in this time, and something better is on the horizon."

At the time that advice seemed contrary to anything I was feeling. *Excited?*

Only months later, when we saw all that God did through that time in our lives, did I get it. Not only did we grow closer to the Lord as a family, the job situation turned out to be the catalyst for the best decision we ever made. My husband chose to start his own business, and that was the beginning of a faith journey like never before.

We wouldn't have had the opportunity to grow like we did if God hadn't allowed us to experience that loss and that hardship. So looking back, yes, I count it all joy.

We don't naturally default to joy in a painful time, but the next time you are in a trial, remember the pain you feel after you workout. Remember how it is necessary to build up those muscles, and thank God He is growing you spiritually in all things. Even in the pain. Even in the hardships. Perseverance is produced and there is joy on the other side.

Exodus 20:17

Observation	Interpretation

Application

Exodus 20:17

"You shall not covet your neighbor's house; you shall not covet your neighbor's wife, nor his male servant, nor his female servant, nor his ox, nor his donkey, nor anything that is your neighbor's."

My Notes

Exodus 20:17

My Prayer

_____
_____
_____
_____
_____
_____
_____
_____
_____
_____
_____
_____
_____
_____
_____
_____
_____
_____
_____
_____
_____
_____
_____
_____
_____
_____
_____

Exodus 20:17

A Note from Karen

Do you covet your neighbor's donkey? I am guessing probably not. But do you covet their car? Do you wish your house was as big as theirs? Or as clean? Or as organized? Do you look at other people's things and wish you had them?

Our media-saturated culture has glorified a coveting culture. We don't even realize it but with the advent of HGTV, Pinterest and Instagram, everything promises us a better life with a better home, office, outfit, you name it! And we don't realize it, but we are coveting. Because what we see in the media stirs in us a feeling of inadequacy and ingratitude.

The perfect example of this for me was several years ago after we had moved into our dream home. I was never one to care much about the house or decor but we loved the property our little hobby farm was set on. And mostly, we loved the simple life it allowed us. It wasn't a perfect house, but we knew it was God's gift to us and we were so grateful. I truly love my house!

One night we had just finished watching an episode of "Fixer Upper." We had been in this habit of watching one every night before bed. After about five nights of episodes, we turned off the TV and I looked around my house and thought, *"My house stinks."*

We had no fancy decor. We didn't have beautifully appointed furniture. We were lacking the aesthetics I saw on TV. Everything was plain and simple.

Then I remarked to my husband, "Maybe we need to get one of those farm sinks like they have on the shows. That will really make our home look better." He looked at me like I had three heads. "We have a brand new home, with a brand new kitchen and a perfectly good and working kitchen sink. Karen, you wash *dirty* dishes in the sink!"

He was right. It functioned. It was new. Why would I spend thousands of dollars on a sink I didn't need. The thought never occurred to me that my home wasn't beautiful until I had let those images on TV influence me.

Our culture glorifies coveting because we are a DIY, fixer-upper, make-it-better world these days. You must be grounded in the truth and content with what you have. The world will entice you, but God's Word is more enticing. It is alive and active and soul-transforming!

Are you looking around you and wanting what others have? Choose today, to listen to God and do what He says. Do not covet. Do not want what is not yours. You have all you need in Christ.

Jeremiah 17:5

Observation	Interpretation

Application

Jeremiah 17:5

Thus says the Lord:

"Cursed is the man who trusts in man
And makes flesh his strength,
Whose heart departs from the Lord.

My Notes

Jeremiah 17:5

My Prayer

Jeremiah 17:5

A Note from Karen

It is very easy to get distracted in our world today by so many voices clamoring for our attention. It is hard to hear His voice above all the noise. But sometimes the loudest voice can be our own.

For years I haven been an anxious soul. From a little girl until an adult woman, I can turn over every scenario in my head with the best of them! I can focus on "What if?" far more than "God will!" And I can go down the endless spiral of fear and anxiety in my thoughts.

Years ago, I realized the real sin of all that behavior. I wasn't trusting God and I wasn't really believing His Word. God cares for the entire universe which is far greater than our human minds can grasp. How can I doubt that He cares for me?

I think the problem is, I knew He cared for me, but what if I didn't like the outcome?

God works all things for good (Romans 8:28) even those things that don't feel good. So when we move from a heart set on our flesh and trusting in ourselves, to a heart that is truly set on God, we fully surrender our lives to Him, no matter what the outcome.

We can't surrender only if we agree with the outcome. That isn't true surrender.

We turn from God when we put our trust in ourselves or what we think is best. We must fully submit every single part of our lives to God. He controls every detail of every thing, and He knows more than we do. We only have a sliver of the infinite amount of information He knows. So why would we trust in ourselves?

That is like having a map of my town and trying to navigate the entire world with it!

Our trust is in the Lord alone. When we trust in ourselves and our flesh we will never be truly content, because we are flawed and sinful and we weren't created to be in charge.

But trusting in a perfect God who is omniscient? It's like throwing out that map of the town, knowing the One who has the map of the world is navigating! That is the guide I want to follow.

How about you? Do you find yourself trusting in yourself or in God? Truly trusting Him in every single detail of your life, even if sometimes it doesn't make sense or the outcome doesn't feel good?

Are you able to give up control of your life to the One who created it?

Today, choose to surrender. Truly surrender every single detail. After all, the One who made you, knows exactly where you need to be.

John 10:10

Observation	Interpretation

Application

John 10:10

The thief does not come except to steal, and
to kill, and to destroy. I have come that they
may have life, and that they may have it more
abundantly.

My Notes

John 10:10

My Prayer

_____
_____
_____
_____
_____
_____
_____
_____
_____
_____
_____
_____
_____
_____
_____
_____
_____
_____
_____
_____
_____
_____
_____
_____
_____
_____

John 10:10

A Note from Karen

Have you ever been robbed? Have you ever had something stolen from you? It is quite violating to have something personal taken from you.

But have you ever had your joy stolen? Or your time stolen? Or your peace?

Jesus came to give us life abundantly. Yet, the enemy is constantly on the prowl to steal that from us. He has stolen my joy and I have given way too much of my time to him.

For instance, those nights I have spent worrying over something. The hours and hours I have spent anxious instead of spending time with the Lord. I had my joy, my peace, and my time stolen. The enemy sought, stole, and ultimately wants to destroy.

Jesus didn't die on the cross so we could spend time on the things He has already taken care of. It is human nature to be concerned for things, but it is sin to let concern replace your faith with fear.

When we remember that Jesus gives us all we need, we can put up our defense so when the enemy is prowling around us, we are secure that nothing will be stolen from us and we can never be destroyed.

Now when I wake up with anxious thoughts, I recognize there is an adversary who wants to steal, but I am secure in Christ. I suit up in my armor of God and he is locked out.

The abundant life comes from a secure life knowing you are safe in Him always. He can not steal any longer. He can not kill my soul. He can not destroy me. I am safe in my Father's arms.

The next time you feel the enemy on the prowl in your life, repeat the words, "I am secure in Christ. Forever." He will flee. And you can walk in a life abundantly filled with Jesus.

Matthew 6:19-21

Observation	Interpretation

Application

Matthew 6:19-21

Do not lay up for yourselves treasures on earth, where moth and rust destroy and where thieves break in and steal; but lay up for yourselves treasures in heaven, where neither moth nor rust destroys and where thieves do not break in and steal. For where your treasure is, there your heart will be also.

My Notes

Matthew 6:19-21

My Prayer

_____
_____
_____
_____
_____
_____
_____
_____
_____
_____
_____
_____
_____
_____
_____
_____
_____
_____
_____
_____
_____
_____
_____
_____
_____
_____

Matthew 6:19-21

A Note from Karen

What do you treasure? What do you store up? Many of us hold onto things because it reminds us of a sentimental time or evokes an emotion in us. So we hold on. Even though we may not look at those things often, we are comforted knowing they are still there.

Then there are those who truly do store up. They always want to be prepared. They don't want to run out of anything, so they store and store until their basements and garages are full.

Clutter often makes us feel discontent. A cluttered room stirs up some anxiety. The very things we seek to bring us comfort end up making us feel stressed and chaotic. The endless piles. The cluttered rooms. The stuff that always seems to be there.

I always say I am the opposite of a hoarder. If it is in my way, be warned, at any time I will toss it!

I wasn't always this way. As a little girl I was very messy and a collector of things. But the stress it caused wore me down.

Over the years, God has transformed my thinking and changed my mindset. I don't look to stuff to store anymore, but I look to Him. And I know that nothing here will last. All those childhood trinkets and memories I held onto, eventually got dusty.

But the treasure we store in heaven can never fade. In fact every single thing on this earth is decaying. Do you know that it is an actual property in physics that all matter is constantly breaking down?

Yet if you look at the Christian life...we are in a constant state of sanctification. We move heavenward and upward and only get better, as the stuff around us– the earth and everything in it– is in a constant state of decay. Isn't that amazing? So why do we spend our time and treasure trying to preserve what will not last?

So why hold onto things when we know they are not our true treasure?

What are you storing up? What are you collecting? What are you treasuring? How can you change your perspective today to stop storing on earth and start storing in heaven?

Galatians 1:10

Observation	Interpretation

Application

Galatians 1:10

For do I now persuade men, or God? Or do I seek to please men? For if I still pleased men, I would not be a bondservant of Christ.

My Notes

Galatians 1:10

My Prayer

_____
_____
_____
_____
_____
_____
_____
_____
_____
_____
_____
_____
_____
_____
_____
_____
_____
_____
_____
_____
_____
_____
_____
_____
_____
_____
_____
_____
_____
_____

Galatians 1:10

A Note from Karen

Are you a people pleaser? Do you do things with the intention of what they think of you? Do you serve because you want to get accolades from others? Or look good to others?

We often say yes to serving because it makes us look good and we care what others think. We don't realize how many decisions we make that are rooted in the approval of others and not in honoring God.

There was a time when my husband and I said yes to everything. We served our hearts out. And it didn't take long until we were burnt out and starting to feel resentful. Instead of worshiping on Sunday mornings, we were "on the schedule" in some capacity to serve at church. It felt like we weren't worshiping or serving. We were working. There is a difference.

The red flag was the fact that we were burnt out and complaining. It felt like work and drudgery, not work for the Lord.

If you are complaining about serving you are not truly serving.

We had to take a good look inside our spirit and test our hearts. We were not serving to please God but to please man.

Approval from others is a natural desire of the human heart. And remember, the human heart is sinful. The natural desire to please others really is rooted in pride. We want them to think well of us and we get puffed up when we are recognized.

My husband and I ended up taking a good amount of time off from serving, so that we could take a step back and evaluate our hearts. And repent. We recognized that we were serving in our own strength and for the wrong motive. We weren't saying yes in order to serve the Lord.

We were saying yes because we were afraid to say no.

A heart that is only seeking the approval of God will serve cheerfully and gladly and will serve out of a desire for the Lord. We should not be seeking the applause of man. And I do not believe we are always seeking accolades. But just the notion that we don't say no because we fear how we look to others, is a sign that we aren't wholeheartedly serving the Lord.

Today, evaluate the areas in which you serve. Do they fill you up or deplete you? We all have different areas that we are gifted to serve and no one is made to fill all areas of service. Find your natural bent, your God-given gift, and serve there. Remember, we are not winning awards for who serves more. In fact, God will give us our eternal award because of Jesus, not because of anything we do.

And in the end, if you are truly trying to serve the Lord, you will please people. But your motivation won't be *first* to please them. Instead it is an outflow of your service to the Lord.

Heart work is hard, but always necessary to keep our lives free from anything that gets in the way of truly seeking the Lord.

Ecclesiastes 5:10

Observation	Interpretation

Application

Ecclesiastes 5:10

He who loves silver will not be satisfied with silver;
Nor he who loves abundance, with increase.
This also is vanity.

My Notes

Ecclesiastes 5:10

My Prayer

_____
_____
_____
_____
_____
_____
_____
_____
_____
_____
_____
_____
_____
_____
_____
_____
_____
_____
_____
_____
_____
_____
_____
_____
_____
_____

Ecclesiastes 5:10

A Note from Karen

Have you ever felt really poor? You know when you can't even afford a pizza? How about really rich? You didn't even have to think about the cost, you could order 10 pizzas if you wanted?

Quite frankly, we haven't ever been very impoverished or very wealthy. We have lived with very little and we have also been more comfortable.

I remember saying how we would be happy if we could just make a certain amount of money. And the years passed, and our businesses grew and we finally had achieved it. But it seemed the more we had the more we spent. And our problems were still there. In fact, sometimes more money added more problems.

Because it was never about the money.

It was about our hearts. If you are thinking that wealth will satisfy, it will never be enough.

We watch the show where famous investors are given the opportunity to invest in entrepreneurs, and as we have come to realize these millionaires and billionaires will never have enough. They continue to invest in new things. They continue to find ways to acquire more wealth. One night I said to my family, "If I were them I would just be content with what I have!" I mean they are richer than we could ever imagine and they continue to desire more.

But that's human nature. It was so evident there in the Garden of Eden. It was never enough.

Adam and Eve walked with God and He had provided every thing they would ever need in a paradise. And they wanted more. And we all know how that turned out.

You can be content with very little or content with very much. It has nothing to do with riches if you are content with what God has provided for you.

Evaluate your heart today and ask yourself, if you had unlimited riches right now would you be truly happier? Would your life have more meaning? Or would it cause more problems?

Remember, what you desire in your heart will determine how you live your life. So do not be satisfied in riches. Be satisfied in Jesus.

Psalm 90:12

Observation

Interpretation

Application

Psalm 90:12

So teach us to number our days, That we may gain
a heart of wisdom.

My Notes

Psalm 90:12

My Prayer

_____
_____
_____
_____
_____
_____
_____
_____
_____
_____
_____
_____
_____
_____
_____
_____
_____
_____
_____
_____
_____
_____
_____
_____
_____
_____
_____
_____

Psalm 90:12
A Note from Karen

What will you think someday about the life you are living now? Will you look back when time is running out and realize how much energy and focus you spent on the wrong things?

Will you say you ran well? Or were you running in circles?

I don't know what it is, but lately I have been moved more and more by things the Lord is teaching me. He is showing me what is really important. Showing me the fleetingness of the days. I am changing.

I have always known God should be at the center but more and more I see the huge difference when I operate out of my walk with the Lord and His Word versus when I operate out of my flesh.

The truth is many of us are walking around with our agenda and our hopes and our wants. And then adding God in after we make our plans. I do it too.

And lately I know how different my days are when I live out of my relationship with God trusting in His will in all things. I don't go after my desires and then try to add God in. Instead, I take everything away and operate with Him at the center. Then HE adds in just what I need.

Life is short. And it's not really about the things we think it's about. All this running around, chasing after stuff day after day. Only to feel burnt out and worn out. Unhappy. Tired. Stressed. Or discontent.

Because we've got it backwards. We weren't meant to be out of step with Him. We need to let Him lead. Not knowing what the future holds but Who holds the future. It's a completely different mode of living. And it's the only way I want to live.

I don't know what tomorrow brings, but I know God. He has created every moment and every detail. My only purpose is to walk where He calls. Wherever He calls.

I encourage you today. Walk with Him. Stop trying to get ahead of Him and later asking Him to join you. Stop making plans apart from Him. His will should be your only plan. The days are short. Live with that wisdom, knowing each moment matters.

Surrender to His will and do all things out of your relationship with Him. And watch your life be changed.

Ephesians 6:10

Observation	Interpretation

Application

Ephesians 6:10

Finally, my brethren, be strong in the Lord and in
the power of His might.

My Notes

Ephesians 6:10

My Prayer

_____

_____

_____

_____

_____

_____

_____

_____

_____

_____

_____

_____

_____

_____

_____

_____

_____

_____

_____

_____

_____

_____

_____

_____

_____

_____

_____

_____

Ephesians 6:10

A Note from Karen

Sometimes the Lord takes away, so we can operate in His power alone.

Recently we lost electricity for several days during a snow and ice storm. The first evening, after everyone was asleep, it was just my Bible and me, in the deafening silence by candlelight. And I was brought back to a simpler time when that was normal. Darkness. Stillness. Quiet. And it was peaceful. There was absolutely nothing to distract me. I was alone with my God, there by the soft glow of the candlelight.

There was so much danger outside with ice and trees down. But I felt safe right there. I was grateful to be curled up in my home. Under blankets. With His Word.

The Lord protects. His Word comforts. And I knew that in the morning the light would dawn again. But there in the dark of night I saw the gift I was given. To sit in stillness and quiet and meditate on all He has done. And think about just how great He is.

Sometimes there's so much noise, I don't think about who He is. His voice gets drowned out by the noise of the world. But that night, He had all my attention. And I was brought to tears.

Sometimes the distractions get taken away by force, and when they're gone you realize how precious life is beneath all the noise and worry of this world.

Life gets hard and overwhelming and anxious thoughts start to win. The world gets our full attention. But that night, I was given a new perspective.

The Lord is my Light. Nothing in this world can ever supply the power He does. When all is stripped away, His light shines in the darkness. His power gives us all we need. It's amazing what we actually see when everything else is taken away.

Power. May we always operate knowing He is the one that supplies all we need. It is so easy to rely on ourselves. But we usually fall short. We burn out. We get overwhelmed. We worry. We fear. We run out of power.

Today, remember all you need is Jesus. He never gets overwhelmed or burnt out. He never falls short.

A life lived for Him supplies all the power you need, here, and for eternity.

Thank you Jesus, for saving me. Thank you to my
family for being the greatest gifts from God. And thank
you to all who have supported my work over the years.
All Glory to God!
~Karen

It has been my prayer that this book will point you to Jesus, grow your desire for the Bible, and encourage you daily. I hope it has done just that. If you were blessed by this devotional in any way, would you share it with others? Spread the Word about it and the ministry here at Simply Living for Him. We believe women can change the world when they are women in the Word!

Share a photo with the hashtags
#SLFHDevotional or #LessClutterMoreJoy
We want to see YOUR photo!

Encourage other women to have less clutter and more joy!
It is all about Jesus.

For more encouragement and resources:
Simply Living for Him
www.simplylivingforhim.com

Blogs, Daily Scripture, podcast, resources,
consulting, books, e-courses, and more!

Simply Living for Him on Facebook **@simplylivingforhim**
Simply Living for Him on Instagram **@simplylivingforhim**

The Simply Living for Him Podcast
This popular podcast has been listened to by thousands around the world on six continents. New episodes weekly. Karen shares about all things simple. Life on her hobby farm, homeschooling, and Jesus. Available on your favorites podcast streaming app including iTunes, Google Play, Sound Cloud, Spotify, Stitcher, and more!

For speaking inquiries:
Please contact **karen@simplylivingforhim** or visit
http://simplylivingforhim.com/speaking-opportunities/
for Karen's latest speaking engagements